A BOSTON STORY

A Comedy

by

RONALD GOW

Based on a novel by Henry James

ENGLISH THEATRE GUILD LTD.
Ascot House, 52 Dean Street, London, W.1

PRESS APPRECIATION

" ELOQUENCE AND WIT, AND, HURRAH, IT'S HERE TO STAY. The play tells a good story, employs language that is always a pleasure to hear, and is acted by a cast of amusing and accomplished players." *Sunday Express*.

" A solid, well constructed story, beautifully acted, and featuring a happy ending. This rare specimen of entertainment is called ' A BOSTON STORY '. It is warmly recommended." *Daily Mirror*.

" Eloquence and wit recover some of their lost ground in the West End with a thoroughly well-made new play by Ronald Gow at the Duchess Theatre called ' A BOSTON STORY '." *Sunday Express*.

" Wit and style." *The People*.

" A skilful adaptation." Harold Hobson, *Sunday Times*.

" Very amusing and enjoyable." *Daily Mail*.

" A charming success." John Barber, *Telegraph*.

A BOSTON STORY is based on Henry James's first novel, WATCH AND WARD, written as a serial in 1870 and published in book form in 1878. As it has never been counted among the novelist's more important works, the dramatist has allowed himself a certain freedom in the adaptation. The freedom is similar to that taken by Henry James when he decided to make a play of one of his own novels and wrote in his notebook:

" His proposal is that I shall make a play of *The American*, and there is no doubt a play in it. I must extract the simplest, strongest, baldest, most rudimentary, at once most humorous and most touching one, in a form whose main *souci* shall be pure situation and pure point combined with pure brevity. Oh, how it must not be too good and how very bad it must be! A moi, Scribe; à moi, Sardou, à moi Dennery!"

This play was first produced in 1964 at the Theatre Royal, Windsor with the title *Watch and Ward* and at Birmingham Repertory Theatre in 1966 with the present title. It was presented by Sherwood and Reid and Kellan Productions at the Duchess Theatre, London, on September 19th, 1968, with the following cast.

Roger Lawrence	……………………	Tony Britton
Lucinda Brown	……………	Rosamond Burne
Hubert Lawrence	………………	Basil Hoskins
Isabel Keith	………………………	Dinah Sheridan
Nora Lambert	………………………	Nicola Pagett
George Fenton	…………………	Patrick Mower

Directed by Malcolm Farquhar

Setting by Geoffrey Scott

Lighting by Michael Northen

CHARACTERS
(in order of appearance)

LUCINDA BROWN
ROGER LAWRENCE
HUBERT LAWRENCE
ISABEL KEITH
NORA
GEORGE FENTON

The action takes place in
the Library of Roger's home outside Boston

ACT ONE
Autumn 1877

INTERVAL

ACT TWO
SCENE I *Christmas Eve.*
SCENE II *Early New Year.*

INTERVAL

ACT THREE
SCENE I *Spring of the following year.*
SCENE II *Ten days later*

ACT I

The Library in the house of ROGER LAWRENCE, *outside Boston.*

It is a pleasant room, with tall windows, as befit a New England house with a portico. A garden door or French window gives access to the " piazza". There is a prominent fireplace. Double doors lead to the hall. Surprisingly there is a piano. A writing desk has a globe on it. The room has been given some cosiness by new curtains and cushions.

LUCINDA *enters carrying a vase of flowers. She is a middle-aged Irish housekeeper and at the moment is dressed with bonnet and cape for going outdoors.*

(ROGER LAWRENCE *calls distantly.*)

ROGER. Lucinda! Are you there, Lucinda?
LUCINDA. I'm here, sir.
ROGER. Where?
LUCINDA. In the library. (*She arranges the flowers and mutters loudly to herself.*) *And* I'm minding my own business . . . *and* I'm keeping myself calm . . . *and* I'm not behaving as though it was the second coming itself had descended upon us! For heaven's sake, man . . . keep your hair on!

(ROGER *enters.*)

(*He is an earnest young-old man and may not be unlike the young Henry James. Short-sighted, shy, but precise in manner, dress and speech. " The desire to get the better of his diffidence has given him a certain formalism of manner which many persons found entirely amusing." But he has " a fund of exquisite human expression ". In other words he has considerable charm.*)

ROGER (*entering*). What do you say?

LUCINDA. Nothing, sir. Nothing at all.

ROGER. I thought you spoke.

LUCINDA. I said nothing that concerns nobody except myself.

ROGER. Do you know you have to be at the station in twenty minutes time?

LUCINDA. I know very well, but the train from the North is always late. (*She tidies things.*)

ROGER. It would be calamitous if she was kept waiting.

LUCINDA. It would be nothing of the sort.

ROGER. What's that?

LUCINDA. I said nothing at all. I'm going now. I've never kept her waiting yet.

(ROGER *takes a travelling rug from a chair.*)

ROGER. Here, take this. (*He hands her a rug.*) Wrap it well round her when she sits in the carriage. She may be chilled after the journey.

(*He attempts to fold the rug.*)

LUCINDA. All right. Give it to me. I'll do that.

(*A bell rings.*)

There! That'll be Mr. Hubert now. I'll go.

ROGER. Ask him to come straight in. And please hurry!

(LUCINDA *goes into the hall.*)

(ROGER *adjusts the flowers and then decides to move them to the mantelshelf. Then he braces himself to receive* HUBERT, *who can be heard talking to* LUCINDA *in the hall.*)

HUBERT (*off*). Good morning, Lucinda.

LUCINDA (*off*). Ah, Mr. Hubert! It's nice to see you after all this long time, and welcome to you.

(LUCINDA *can be seen taking his hat and coat.*)

HUBERT. Thank you, Lucinda, thank you. And how are you?

LUCINDA. I'm as well as can be expected, sir, with all the comings and goings. It's Mr. Hubert, sir.

ROGER. Show him in.

(HUBERT *comes into the room. He is " extremely good-looking and clever", and younger than* ROGER. *There is a slight awkwardness in the meeting.*)

Ah, Hubert . . . !

HUBERT. Roger . . . !

(*They shake hands.* HUBERT *makes for the fire.*)

LUCINDA. I'll be going now, sir.

ROGER. Yes, please go. And hurry!

(LUCINDA *goes, closing the doors. After another awkward moment of silence* ROGER *waves to a chair.*)

Do sit down. Did you have a good journey?

HUBERT. Excellent, thank you.

ROGER. Very good of you to come all this way. And at such short notice too.

HUBERT. Yes, it was.

(*He surveys the room and the flowers surprise him.*)

ROGER. Rather a long time, wasn't it?

HUBERT. Two years. We quarrelled, didn't we?

ROGER. No, no! That was nothing. I lost my temper. Don't talk about that. I've been round the world since then. You see, Hubert, I want to ask your opinion.

HUBERT. My dear Roger, I'm delighted.

ROGER. You know what it's about.

HUBERT. I think so. What made you do it in the first place?

ROGER. It's an odd story.

HUBERT. Damned odd!

ROGER. Pray be seated. (HUBERT *sits and* ROGER *clears his throat.*) Hubert—I want you to know that I respect your opinion. Very much indeed. There were times in the past when I was angry with you. That was because I was afraid of you.

HUBERT. Afraid?

ROGER. I admit it. You may be some years my junior . . .

HUBERT. Two.

ROGER. But you always seemed to me to be so infernally clever. So—*trenchant* in your opinions. So unconventional, so upsetting . . . in short not to put too fine a point on it,

I've always felt that, you were, may I say? — *laughing* at me.

HUBERT.   Perhaps you needed it.

ROGER.   Possibly. But I do take you seriously. And I need advice. And if you do say something, and make me angry . . . I want you to be patient with me.

(ROGER *sits*.)

HUBERT.   Of course I'll be patient with you. What I fail to understand is why you are needing my opinion after all these years. We felt at the time you were rather secretive about it, you know. It was two whole years before you permitted any of us to see her and pass judgement on her. When men behave like that one is inclined to scrutinise their motives. When I asked you where she came from and who she was and what you knew about her you lost your temper with me.

ROGER.   You said she had big feet.

HUBERT.   I was inclined to think so.

ROGER.   That was because I made her wear big shoes. She has beautiful feet and I intended that they should remain so.

HUBERT.   Actually what I said was that she had *les pieds enormes*. I said it in French so that she wouldn't understand.

ROGER.   *I* understood.

HUBERT.   I'm sorry. I didn't know you were so proud of her feet.

ROGER.   I hope you will be able to revise your opinion of her.

HUBERT.   I hope so too.

(HUBERT *takes a cigar from his case*.)

ROGER (*rising*).   You're not smoking!

HUBERT.   Why? Do you object?

ROGER.   Not in here.

HUBERT.   I'm sorry. In that case I wouldn't dream of it.

ROGER.   Not in this room. Not today. I don't want to have the air polluted.

HUBERT.   Oh!

ROGER (*crossing to French window*).   We can go out on the piazza, if you wish.

HUBERT. Oh, no, no. I can do without, thank you.

(*He laughs as he puts the cigar away.*)

ROGER. Why are you laughing?

HUBERT. You call it the " piazza "?

ROGER. Why not?

HUBERT. In New York we call it the porch.

ROGER. Porch!

HUBERT. There you have the essential difference between the Bostonian and the New Yorker. The piazza and the porch.

ROGER. Don't think I'm against smoking. (*He smiles.*) I recently acquired the habit myself.

(ROGER *crosses to fire.*)

HUBERT. Did you!

ROGER. On my journey round the world.

HUBERT. You're quite an old devil, aren't you?

ROGER. I limit myself, of course.

HUBERT. Of course. And now you've acquired a young woman.

ROGER. I will not have her called a young woman! She is a child. An adopted child.

HUBERT. Where is she?

ROGER. She returns today from school.

HUBERT. I see.

ROGER. I believe she is old enough now to leave school altogether.

HUBERT. Ah . . .

ROGER. What do you mean—ah?

HUBERT. Oh, just—ah. A rumination, simply.

ROGER. I have sent Lucinda to our local station to meet her.

(ROGER *looks at watch.*)

HUBERT. Dear old Lucinda! I see she's still with you.

ROGER. She is.

HUBERT. In spite of the adopted child?

ROGER. *Because* of the adopted child.

HUBERT. Really?

ROGER. Lucinda is secretly afraid that I shall marry— bring another woman into the house, and threaten her

supremacy in the kitchen. But to bring Nora into the house
was a good compromise. It meant new carpets and curtains
—and new power for Lucinda. Women like power.

HUBERT. The reason we both remain bachelors, I
suppose.

ROGER. Possibly. We all like freedom.

HUBERT. Am I to draw up some document? Make the
adoption legal?

ROGER. I didn't invite you as a lawyer.

HUBERT. In that case I suppose I get no fee.

ROGER. I sent for you because you're my cousin. When
Nora returns I want her to feel that this *is* her home. I
want her to know she has a family.

HUBERT. A family! You can't adopt for other people.
I shall wait till I see her again. If she's pleasing I shall
admit her into cousinship.

ROGER. I know you think it's comical.

HUBERT. It has its funny side.

ROGER. This is very serious.

HUBERT. I know. Adoption is not to be lightly undertaken. But then you would never take anything lightly,
would you, Roger?

ROGER. More than that. I think I obeyed a divine
command.

HUBERT. Good heavens!

ROGER. I told you about the hotel in New York.

HUBERT. Yes, where you were accosted by her father.
A bit of a scoundrel. He tried to borrow money. Then he
shot himself—committed suicide.

ROGER. He asked me for a loan of a hundred dollars. I
refused him.

HUBERT. Quite right.

ROGER. It has been on my conscience ever since.

HUBERT. Oh, these Bostonian consciences!

ROGER. As you know I am not without money.

HUBERT. No, by Jove! It all went to your side of the
family. All we got was the brains.

ROGER. Hubert—something else happened in that hotel
that night.

HUBERT. Something else on your conscience!

ROGER. I have nothing whatever to be ashamed of!

HUBERT. What a wasted life!

ROGER. I went to that hotel to meet a woman.

HUBERT. Don't tell me anything you're going to regret, will you?

ROGER. Hubert, I am serious. I was desperate.

HUBERT. Ah?

ROGER. I went to offer marriage to her—for the last time. She refused me. She sailed that night for Europe. Within minutes of parting from her this little child—Nora—had flung herself into my arms. Her father had blown his brains out upstairs in his bedroom. I believe it was one of those strange acts we call Providence.

HUBERT. Providence seems to have been reckless that night.

ROGER. From that moment I never thought again of the woman I had loved so desperately. All that passion and fury were gone. As if they had never been. Every thought I had was centred on Nora. It was as though—in a manner of speaking—she had been given to me as a compensation for what I had lost. Do you follow?

HUBERT. I follow.

ROGER. I brought her home. I got rid of the dogs. I rebuilt this house for her. I taught her to read and write. I even set to work to educate myself in order that I could educate her. That is why I have been round the world. (*Crosses to desk.*) I have a pile of notebooks there. I shall study them with her. I want to share with her all the wonderful things I have seen and done. Now she has left school I shall endeavour to lay the foundation of her culture.

HUBERT. What happened to the woman who sailed for Europe?

ROGER. Isabel! Oh, she went to Rome and married the man of her choice. She did as many Americans do and entered the Roman Catholic Church. In spite of her prayers her husband died. He left her—and the Church—well provided for.

HUBERT. A wealthy widow?

ROGER. She is, I believe, incredibly rich. She is also coming here today.

HUBERT (*rising*). My dear fellow, why didn't you tell me?

ROGER. I have told you.

HUBERT. This is undoubtedly the problem on which you require my opinion.

ROGER. There is no problem. I have invited her for the same reason I invited you. To be here when Nora comes home. She is my nearest neighbour.

HUBERT (*taking Roger's hand*). Am I not to congratulate you? Don't you mean that Providence, on which you so greatly rely, has brought you together again?

ROGER. Certainly not! Just because she happened to come and live in a house nearby. It never entered my head. Nor hers either.

HUBERT. I wouldn't be too sure.

ROGER. She is, of course, very attractive.

HUBERT. Ah!

ROGER (*coldly*). But she is simply my neighbour.

HUBERT (*softly*). Love thy neighbour!

ROGER. I tell you all the past is dead. Besides, I have even been in love with another woman since then.

HUBERT. Where?

ROGER. In South America.

HUBERT. Beautiful?

ROGER. Perfection. A sweet and lovely Peruvian girl.

HUBERT. Why on earth didn't you marry her and bring her home?

ROGER. Because I felt my duty was here.

HUBERT. Beside the wealthy widow?

ROGER. No! No!

HUBERT. And you wish me to be your spokesman?

ROGER. No, no, no!

HUBERT. Then where do I come in?

ROGER. I need you. You're a man of the world—a New Yorker. That sardonic tongue of yours might keep me from making a fool of myself. Even if you do make me angry.

HUBERT. I shall do my duty, I hope.

ROGER. You promise that?

HUBERT. As a lawyer? Or as a man of the world? It isn't always the same thing you know.

ROGER. I want your honest opinion. About this adoption.

HUBERT. Very well. How old is Nora now?

ROGER. Sixteen.

HUBERT (*picking up a framed photograph*). Hm?

ROGER. Why do you say " Hm "?

HUBERT. That's how I remember her. **A child.**

ROGER. Very pretty, isn't she?

HUBERT. I'd say *striking*.

ROGER. I say *pretty*!

HUBERT. Very well. I never thought of her as a girl. She seemed more like a boy—climbing trees and keeping rabbits. When did you see her last?

ROGER. Before I went abroad.

HUBERT. A child grows rapidly. Suddenly a young woman emerges.

ROGER. Everything is arranged for her in a very seemly manner. I have Lucinda to look after her. I have Isabel and yourself to advise me. I hope you're not suggesting . . .

HUBERT. I'm suggesting nothing. I'm advising. What are you going to do when she's eighteen? Seventeen, for that matter. They say girls mature earlier than ever.

ROGER. That is something the young woman will have to settle for herself. I want to give her every freedom. Freedom of choice—freedom of intellect—freedom of livelihood . . .

(*A bell rings.*)

This will be Isabel. Please remember her married name—Mrs. Keith.

(*He suddenly remembers.*)

Oh! I must go. Lucinda's at the station. Forgive me. And remember—there is no longer anything between us.

(*ROGER goes.*)

HUBERT. So you say!

(HUBERT *shakes his head and replaces the photograph.* ROGER *is heard opening the front door and greeting* ISABEL. *He returns with her. She is good-looking, stylish and assured.*)

ROGER (*in hall*). Isabel, my dear, you're welcome—and how well you're looking! . . . It is so good of you to come . . .

ISABEL (*appearing in hall*). I'm delighted! Is she here yet?

ROGER. No, not arrived yet. Lucinda's gone to the station to meet her. (*He looks at his watch.*) I imagine we shall see them any moment now. Please come in. Hubert! I beg your pardon. This is my cousin, Hubert Lawrence. From New York. This is my friend and neighbour, Mrs. Keith.

ISABEL (*offering her hand*). How do you do, Mr. Lawrence?

HUBERT. How do you do, Mrs. Keith? I'm very happy to make your acquaintance.

(*He shakes her hand.*)

ISABEL. Roger never told me he had a New Yorker in the family.

HUBERT. He is, I believe, ashamed of me.

ROGER. Hubert has a law practice.

ISABEL. How useful!

HUBERT. Criminal law.

ISABEL. One never knows. Does one? Look—the new curtains! Did you choose them? (*She inspects them.*)

ROGER. Yes. Do you like them?

ISABEL. And the carpet too! Look! How this room has changed!

ROGER. You like it?

ISABEL. Most elegant!

ROGER. I hope not without regard for taste. You do admire the taste?

ISABEL. Of course. It's impeccable. But . . .

ROGER. There's something wrong?

ISABEL. I used to know this room as a bachelor's apartment—all mahogany and old leather and horsehair. Now it's all so light. Chintz and muslin—flowers—photographs—new curtains—and a piano too!

ROGER. That's for Nora to learn music on. I hope she's going to like it.

ISABEL. Nora is a very lucky girl.

ROGER. I have built a small new wing where she has her bedroom. I must show you.

HUBERT. I hope she's grateful, that's all.

ROGER (*watching* ISABEL, *who is scrutinising the curtain*). Is anything wrong? You don't think I've carried the decorations too far? You know I have a horror of wanton luxury. You think it's over-done?

ISABEL. I just wondered . . .

ROGER. What?

ISABEL. Chintz and muslin . . . ? In Winter?

ROGER. I thought something virginal—something propitious for a young girl.

ISABEL (*laughing*). Dear Roger!

ROGER. What's wrong?

ISABEL. I see you are trying to be father and mother too.

ROGER. I must. She has nobody. No home. No background. I am trying to furnish her little world. So empty.

ISABEL. It's all done with great discretion, Roger. I was just thinking that the old ancestral relics—the old furniture—the musty smell—that was part of your home too. That was what you had to offer her. Something masculine. All your male ancestors looking down from their portraits—and frowning slightly. . . .

ROGER. I threw them out.

ISABEL. You may need them. We all need something to frighten us.

HUBERT. As we need the Old Testament. The old admonitory gods.

ROGER (*angrily turning away*). Oh, very well! I can tell you don't like it. Either of you.

ISABEL. But I do, Roger, I do!

HUBERT. You did ask for our advice.

ROGER. I beg your pardon. Forgive me. I know you both mean well. I'll have the family portraits hung on the stairs. In the dark. (*He looks at the books on the desk.*) These books should have been placed in her room. I selected them myself. "The Heir of Redclyffe", "Henry Esmond", "Selected Poems" . . . no *not* "Jane Eyre", I think. Not yet. (*He puts it aside.*) No. These I am going to put on a little shelf beside her bed. When she opens her eyes in the morning she shall see only good literature. I mean to surround her with beautiful things. Pardon me, I'll put them there before she comes. Hubert, pray entertain Mrs. Keith.

(ROGER *goes with the books.*)

HUBERT (*rolling his eyes*). Well!

ISABEL. We shall have to be careful what we say.

HUBERT. I have noticed that.

ISABEL. You and I seem to have a difficult task. What are we? Godparents? Or uncles and aunts?

HUBERT. When Roger is devoted to an ideal, he is very single-minded.

ISABEL. Don't I know it?

HUBERT. You were the ideal once.

ISABEL. I'm afraid so.

HUBERT. May I say that the sooner you become his ideal again the better for all concerned.

ISABEL. Really, Mr. Lawrence!

HUBERT. You think me impertinent?

ISABEL. I hardly expected match-making.

HUBERT. I claim the privilege of being the family lawyer. You mustn't take offence.

ISABEL. I'm afraid that's all over.

HUBERT. I know Roger proposed marriage to you.

ISABEL. Often. He made quite a hobby of it. At the most inconvenient times too. Once at the dentist's. Another time at a funeral. And on the night when I was sailing for Europe.

HUBERT. I can quite understand his persistence now I've seen you. I shall advise him to persevere.

ISABEL. Oh, no!

HUBERT. I wonder if he knows how much he needs you?

ISABEL. Perhaps I am not available.

HUBERT. I think some inner voice has told him. That's why he has invited you today.

ISABEL. This is very flattering, Mr. Lawrence.

HUBERT. I detect the fumes of smouldering ardour. Watch out! He may burst into flame at any moment.

ISABEL. Not after all this time, surely?

HUBERT. Roger is still devoted to you.

ISABEL. In friendship only.

HUBERT. You *had* considered the possibility then—of more than friendship?

ISABEL. Every woman considers every possibility—with every man.

HUBERT. Ah, really?

ISABEL. Every acceptable man, Mr. Lawrence.

HUBERT (*laughing off the slight repulse*). Oh . . . How fortunate you are, Mrs. Keith.

ISABEL. Am I? Why?

HUBERT. You are not only one of the most beautiful women I have ever met. You are also one of the wittiest. You're certainly the wealthiest.

ISABEL. How do you know?

HUBERT. Roger told me.

ISABEL. So he *has* discussed me?

HUBERT. He told me everything. I'm afraid Roger is a little tongue-tied where women are concerned.

ISABEL. Which you are not, Mr. Lawrence.

HUBERT. A certain eloquence is part of my profession.

ISABEL. Are you for me or against me?

HUBERT. Oh, *for* you most definitely! Dear lady, I am at your feet.

ISABEL. That is very comforting.

HUBERT. May I put into words what I imagine Roger sees in you?

ISABEL. Certainly. As long as you keep within the bounds of entertainment, Mr. Lawrence.

HUBERT. I promise that. You see, quite apart from your beauty and your charm and your wealth, there is a strangely mysterious quality about you. Something which very few American women possess. I don't quite know what to call it. It's a poise—an attitude of mind, a style, a nuance. Something they have in Europe. But instead of making you forbidding, as so many European women are, you have kept your native warmth. I think you are the most desirable of women.

ISABEL. Is this speech addressed to the jury, or to me personally?

HUBERT. I am speaking on behalf of my client . . .

ISABEL. Your client?

HUBERT. I mean my cousin. These are the things that I think he ought to say.

ISABEL. Thank you. I'm sure you make a very good advocate.

HUBERT. Oh, yes?

ISABEL. The sort of lawyer I would rather have on my side than against me!

HUBERT. Ha, yes!

ISABEL. Because I think you are a very dangerous man, Mr. Hubert Lawrence.

HUBERT. Dangerous?

ISABEL. I haven't travelled about Europe without being a good judge of character. I am extremely suspicious of that eloquence of which you are so proud.

HUBERT. Oh, really, Mrs. Keith!

ISABEL. Don't you think you ought to let Roger speak for himself?

HUBERT. I want you to know what I am sure is in his heart. I want him to make a good impression.

ISABEL. I am perfectly capable of forming my own impressions, thank you.

HUBERT. I'm sure you are, but don't you see I'm pleading for Roger?

ISABEL. Of course it *is* for Roger, isn't it?

(HUBERT *laughs*.)

HUBERT. Of course. But I believe in all sincerity that he means to make a proposal of marriage to you. He may be slow, he may be tongue-tied. But please be merciful. Think of him, a bachelor with a young girl on his hands. What is he to do?

ISABEL. I'm sure you have a very winning way with juries.

HUBERT. Yes, I believe I have.

ISABEL. But not with *me,* Mr. Lawrence!

(*A door bell rings.*)

ROGER (*off*). Here she is!

(ROGER *enters excitedly.*)

She's here! They've arrived! The carriage is at the door. Listen—I suggest you remain seated in here, and I'll go and open the door. (ISABEL *rises*.) No, Isabel, you . . . if you please . . . remain here.

HUBERT. Shall I go? (*rises*)

ROGER. No (HUBERT *sits again*) . . yes! That would be more suitable. I'll be waiting in here, with Isabel. You and I, Isabel . . . do be seated, please.

(*The bell rings again.*)

There she is! All right, Hubert, you go. Don't keep her waiting.

(HUBERT *goes*. ROGER *crosses to the fire.*)

I caught a glimpse of her through the window, Isabel. Quite miraculous! You've no idea how she's improved. She sat in the carriage, bolt upright, like a princess!

NORA (*off*). Home! Home at last!

ROGER. Hush! Here she is!

(ROGER *stands waiting.* HUBERT *opens the door and* NORA
runs in and embraces ROGER *in a long fierce kiss.*)

(HUBERT *follows with* LUCINDA.)

NORA. Roger! Oh, Roger! Roger! Roger!

ROGER. My dear . . . my dear girl! Welcome . . . welcome
home . . . Ah! There . . . wonderful to see you. . . .

(*He breaks the embrace and turns her round.* HUBERT *crosses
down* R.)

There's Mrs. Keith. Say how do you do. She's come here
especially to meet you.

NORA. How do you do, Mrs. Keith.

ISABEL. How do you do, Nora? How nice to see you. I
hope you're well.

NORA. Thank you. Yes. Very well.

ROGER. You remember cousin Hubert?

NORA. How do you do?

HUBERT. How do you do, little cousin? Aren't you going
to kiss me? (*Nora runs and kisses* HUBERT.) Thank you. Not
so little either, is she. Can this really be Nora?

NORA. Yes, it is. I have been growing up hard since I
saw you. (*She puts out a foot.*) I have had to catch up with
those *pieds enormes. Voila, monsieur*!

LUCINDA. Ah, she speaks French! Bless her!

NORA. I know cousin Hubert said some part of me was
enormous. As soon as they gave me a dictionary I looked up
les pieds. I found it meant the feet.

ROGER. She certainly has caught up with them now, hasn't
she?

HUBERT. I should never have known her. She is an enormous young lady.

NORA. Enormous?

HUBERT. *Formidable*! That is what the French say.

ROGER. Isabel, isn't it a remarkable change?

ISABEL. A change for the better I think.

NORA. Thank you, Mrs. Keith.

HUBERT. No longer a little hoyden—climbing trees.

NORA. I still love climbing trees.

ROGER. Nonsense.

NORA.   I saw my pony in the paddock. Can I go riding?

LUCINDA.   No, Mr. Roger, I think her first duty is to go to her room.

ISABEL.   Just one moment, please, Lucinda. Come here—let me look at you. Did you have a nice journey?

NORA.   Yes, Mrs. Keith, thank you.

ISABEL.   What are you going to do with yourself now?

NORA.   I don't know. I must work I suppose.

ISABEL.   Why?

NORA.   I must do something to repay Roger.

ISABEL.   I see. What kind of work?

NORA.   I could scrub floors. I could look after babies of course.

ISABEL.   Whose babies?

NORA.   Roger's. That is if he has any.

(ROGER *faintly protests*. HUBERT *laughs*.)

I hope he does.

LUCINDA.   Holy Mother of God! What will she say next?

NORA.   Have I said something wrong?

ISABEL.   Of course not. But we must get him married first, mustn't we?

NORA.   That's what I meant. He is extremely marriageable, don't you think?

ISABEL.   Of course. What have they been teaching you at school?

NORA.   Not much. I'm afraid I wasn't very good at school work, Mrs. Keith.

ISABEL.   You spoke a little French just now.

NORA.   A very little.

ISABEL.   Would you like to learn?

NORA.   Very much. Whenever Roger and Cousin Hubert say something I'm not supposed to understand, they say it in French.

ISABEL.   How about other things? Geography, arithmetic?

NORA.   Very bad, Mrs. Keith, very bad.

ISABEL.   How's that?

NORA (*quoting*).   "I lack the power of concentrated effort and do not at all times apply that diligence appropriate to one who should be grateful for the assistance and charity she has received from others."

ISABEL.   Who said that?

Nora. The headmistress. I had to write it out five hundred times.

Roger. Idiotic woman. Teaching methods are all wrong.

Isabel. All the same, Nora, you must learn some arithmetic. I think every American woman should learn how to count her change. Especially if she travels in Europe.

Nora. Yes, Mrs. Keith.

Isabel. And now I think you ought to do what Lucinda says, and go to your room?

Nora. My new room, is it ready?

Roger. Yes, quite ready.

Nora. May I see it? Have you seen it, Cousin Hubert?

Hubert. No.

Nora. May I take Hubert and show him?

Roger. Hubert? Certainly. If you wish . . .

Nora. You would like to see it, wouldn't you?

Hubert. That's very agreeable of you. (*Rises.*)

Lucinda. May I remind you that a cold collation is laid out in the dining-room.

Roger. Oh, yes, of course. We're all going to sit down to some refreshment. It's a party.

Nora. A party!

Roger. In your honour, Nora!

Nora (*jumping*). Ya-hoo!

Lucinda. Be quiet now!

Roger. Don't be long. And, Nora . . .

Nora. Yes?

Roger. I don't think you ought to say " Ya-hoo! " Not now.

Nora. No, Roger. I won't say Ya-hoo. Not any more. Oh, I'm afraid this is my report. From the headmistress.

Roger. Thank you.

(Nora *hands over the report and follows* Lucinda.)

(Hubert *follows, closing the door.*)

Roger (*opening the envelope*). Excuse me, this is her school report.

(*He sits at his desk.*)

Isabel. You let Hubert go with her?

Roger. Why not? I want him to be one of the family. Just like yourself. What do you think of her?

ISABEL (*rising*). Mr. Lawrence, I'm jealous.

ROGER. Truly?

ISABEL. Truly.

ROGER. Not in any way—how shall I put it?—you don't find in her any suggestion of commonness?

ISABEL. I think she's one in a thousand.

ROGER. Plain or pretty, would you say?

ISABEL. She has a style of her own.

ROGER. A touch of the *gamine*, perhaps.

ISABEL. Possibly. She has a kind of way. It's a way that may lead her far. You'll have to watch out.

ROGER. I intend to.

(*He reads the report.*)

(*She looks in a mirror on the piano.*)

ISABEL. How faded it makes one feel!

ROGER. Surely not!

ISABEL. I can't hide the wrinkles on my brow any longer.

ROGER. If there are any—which I very much doubt. Time has stood still with you. Like Joshua's sun, in the heavens.

ISABEL. You still make gallant speeches!

ROGER. Widowhood has agreed with you. Perhaps good works have illuminated your person. Forgive me. (*He looks again at the report in his hand.*)

ISABEL. You speak very kindly, sir.

ROGER. Good heavens! The impertinence! This is what her schoolmistress says. " She has made little progress in deportment and decorum and cannot overcome the handicap of her lowly origin." (*He crumples it up.*) That finishes school! You don't think there's any truth in it, do you?

ISABEL. Nothing that can't be remedied. Nature never meant her to hold up her head so well for nothing.

ROGER. She does hold it well, doesn't she? Could she be a beauty?

ISABEL. She could, very well.

ROGER. You must teach her how to do her hair.

ISABEL. Oh, to have that head of hair and be only sixteen! To have health and a good complexion! It's the very best thing in the world if they did but know it. But do they? No! At that age they must leave it all behind them —they must pull their hair to pieces—they must be twenty.

And before long they must have lovers and go their own gait.

ROGER. We must teach her to be wise.

ISABEL. Do you think you can?

ROGER. Of course. She is most amenable.

ISABEL. When men undertake to meddle with a young girl's education they usually make a fiasco of it.

ROGER (*rising*). Did you say *fiasco*?

ISABEL. You can never be stern enough. Men behave like the veriest old grandmothers where girls are concerned. You need a woman to help you.

ROGER. I have Lucinda.

ISABEL. Yes. You have Lucinda.

ROGER. You must remember it was I who taught her to read and cipher. She knew nothing when she first came here. She uttered words and phrases that were impolite, to say the least of it. She had a passion for strong green tea and the romances in the Sunday newspapers.

ISABEL. I also have a fancy for the Sunday newspapers.

ROGER. I have changed all that. You must remember she springs from vulgar soil. We must be constantly vigilant.

ISABEL. Give her to me for a year and I'll promise you the most charming girl in America.

ROGER. I rely on you. In fact I have enlisted you. But you mustn't take her away from me.

ISABEL. You have a plan?

ROGER. I have a plan.

ISABEL. Am I part of it?

ROGER. You are an important part of it. Pray be seated.

(ISABEL *sits.*)

Isabel—you will of course be aware that my inheritance has left me most comfortably situated. I mean in the matter of worldly goods, and this estate and all that kind of thing. I know that you yourself are a wealthy woman and that money matters very little to you.

ISABEL. Oh, but it does. It can make marriage bearable, and widowhood almost desirable.

ROGER. I am serious, Isabel.

ISABEL. I am sorry, Roger.

ROGER. I have something of importance to tell you. It is an essential part of my plan. You see, I have drawn up a rigid schedule for Nora's future. A table of rules and observances. Now that she has left school I wish to begin her education. I have prepared myself. I have undertaken a course of useful reading—hygiene, morals, history, philosophy —and of course my recent travels in foreign parts give a unique opportunity for the study of geography.

ISABEL. Why, Roger, she'll be a blue-stocking!

ROGER. She will, I hope, be a very remarkable woman.

ISABEL. Very remarkable.

ROGER. I'm afraid I may have lost touch with her during these years at school. When she first came here she thought me—as one might say—omniscient. She thought me—so to speak—infallible. She had enormous confidence in me. I have now to regain that confidence.

ISABEL. I know. You want to be the perfect father. Isn't that it?

ROGER. Did you say " father "?

ISABEL. It's only natural.

ROGER. No, no—not quite.

ISABEL. Why not?

ROGER. Isabel. I have something to tell you. I have told no one else. And of course Nora knows nothing about it.

ISABEL. I think I understand.

ROGER. You've guessed?

ISABEL. Your cousin gave me some little inkling of what you might say.

ROGER. What has he been saying?

ISABEL. He spoke on your behalf. I said I would sooner hear it from your own lips.

ROGER. Quite right. It is a very delicate matter.

ISABEL. You can speak freely, Roger. I don't think there need be any cause for shyness between old friends.

ROGER. This will put us on rather a different footing.

ISABEL. I think I understand.

ROGER. Isabel, what I have to tell you is this. It is not altogether as a father that I see myself.

ISABEL. What then?

ROGER. When Nora is older—in a few years from now— I hope she will be grateful enough not to refuse me as you did.

ISABEL. Roger! Do you mean . . . ?

ROGER. I mean—to marry her. That is my intention. That

is of course, if she's agreeable. She knows nothing. She is young, she is innocent. But I believe a woman can learn to fall in love with a man.

ISABEL. That's what you said to me once.

ROGER. And you wouldn't believe it. Now I have begun at the beginning. I shall train her. I shall bring her up and so guide her mind that she will, of her own free choice, accept me as a husband.

ISABEL. She's only a child.

ROGER. At the moment. An adorable child. But it will be my own fault if she does not grow up to be a perfect wife.

ISABEL. Good heavens!

ROGER. I want her to be the new American woman—free, independent, intellectual. We live in a modern age. This is Boston, 1877. I want her to be like yourself, Isabel—well-travelled, broad-minded, level-headed. . . .

ISABEL. Thank you, sir.

ROGER. In short, I want her to be a woman of the world. Like yourself. And I mean that in no loose or licentious connection.

(She rises and turns to the fire.)

ISABEL. I'm glad of that. Thank you. It's extraordinary!

(She turns on him.)

ROGER. Why extraordinary?

ISABEL. I have heard of men who shot themselves, after a refusal. Or married another. Or even took to drink. But never of one who adopted a girl-child to make her into the perfect wife. Supposing she hates the sight of you?

ROGER. It is a risk I must take. She must choose for herself and go her own way. I shall give her a good dowry.

ISABEL. Supposing she loves you madly—and you hate the sight of her.

ROGER. These violent extremes are unlikely.

ISABEL. But she is a woman.

ROGER. I hope to teach her the art of reason—of equanimity—of philosophy.

ISABEL. Poor child!

ROGER. The ancient Greeks were capable of these virtues and had little trouble with their women.

ISABEL. If you behave like an ancient Greek in Boston you may have other troubles.

ROGER. It will be a great experiment.

ISABEL. And where do I come in?

ROGER. You? That is what I want to ask you. Will you undertake to instruct the girl on Thursday afternoons in the arts of needlework and deportment?

ISABEL. Yes. Certainly. By all means. Is that all?

ROGER. That is all.

(ISABEL *starts to laugh*.)

What are you laughing at?

ISABEL. It's really rather funny . . . ! Oh, Roger! (*She laughs helplessly*.)

(*A gong sounds*.)

ROGER. There—that's Lucinda calling us. Shall we go to the party? (*He offers his arm to* ISABEL.) I understand there is to be ice-cream.

(ISABEL *stands still*.)

What's the matter? You look surprised!

ISABEL. I have never been more surprised in my life!

ROGER. Don't you like ice-cream?

ISABEL. Yes, Roger. I am very fond of ice-cream.

ROGER. Well then, come along.

(*He offers his arm*.)

I need your help.

(*She takes his arm*.)

ISABEL. I think you do!

(*They are going to the door*.)

CURTAIN

END OF ACT ONE

ACT II

SCENE 1

Some weeks later. Christmas Eve.

A single oil-lamp and the glow from the fire illuminate the left half of the room. Heavy curtains are drawn.

ROGER *sits reading from one of his notebooks.* NORA *is binding Christmas garlands from twigs and placing them about the walls. At this moment she is perched on the library steps hanging one above the fireplace.*

NORA *pays divided attention.*

ROGER (*reading*). " Having taken ship in the West Indies, we set sail round the coast of South America, where we were fortunate in finding many opportunities for going ashore and studying the manners and customs of the natives. During this visit to Patagonia . . ." (*He looks up and sees her busy with a garland.*) " During this visit to Patagonia . . ." Nora!

(*She hastily dismounts and runs to the globe on the table.*)

NORA. Sorry! Did you say Patagonia?
ROGER. I did.

(*She examines the globe and puts her finger on the spot.*)

NORA. There.
ROGER. Quite right.

(*She goes to her chair and works on another garland.*)

NORA. Does it trouble you that I'm making these garlands?
ROGER. No. Not much.
NORA. This is the last.
ROGER. Good.

NORA. What time will Cousin Hubert be here, do you think?

ROGER. Hubert? I don't know. (*He reads again.*) " During this visit to Patagonia the captain permitted us to go ashore and I had the exceptional privilege of inspecting a Patagonian village at close quarters. The unhappy denizens of the wild forests of Patagonia have many ancient tribal customs over which it will be fitting that I should draw a veil and not offend the susceptibilities of my readers." Be careful!

(NORA *has climbed up.*)

NORA. I'm listening. Truly. " Tribal customs."

(ROGER *closes the book.*)

ROGER. No. This diary is dull. Terribly dull.

NORA. No, it's not, Roger.

ROGER. I ought to throw it on the fire.

NORA. You must do no such thing. You must print it in a book. Bound in morocco and gilt.

ROGER. I did think of sending it to a publisher, once. Someday I shall take up writing seriously. (*He puts it aside.*) I shall smoke now.

NORA. Yes, Roger.

(NORA *brings a tray on which are some pipes, tobacco, matches and a smoking cap. She puts the cap on his head and then proceeds to fill the pipe. She gives it to him. He lights his pipe. She takes a pack of cards from her work-basket and sits. She flicks the cards noisily.*)

ROGER. What have you there?

NORA. Cards. (*She shuffles expertly.*) Would you like a game?

ROGER (*puffing his pipe*). I do not play cards, Nora.

NORA. I could teach you how to play poker. How to win, too.

ROGER. No, thank you.

NORA. Very well. I'll show you a trick. (*She rises to* L *of* ROGER.) Take a card, please. (*He does.*) Well, look at it. (*He does and shows it to her.*) No! No! You mustn't show me. Put it back. Take another one. Look at it. Remember it. Now put it back. Anywhere. Now then. Abracadabra! There! Is that the card?

ROGER. Good heavens! Yes. As a matter of fact, it is. Who taught you to do that?

NORA. My father. This was his special pack of cards. I keep it in my work-basket. In memory of him.

ROGER. Did he play much—your father?

NORA. In St. Louis some people called him Five Ace Jack.

ROGER. Indeed? There are, I believe, only four aces in a pack.

NORA. My father was never short of aces. You see, he had this pack made specially for cutting. (*She cuts the pack several times on the table beside him.*) See, every time an ace. Do you know how it's done? Feel the edge of the cards, Roger. The aces are all a little larger. Isn't that clever? (*He tries it.*) There you are—you've done it. Every time.

ROGER. Good heavens! Give me the cards. This is sharp practice. You are never to do this sort of thing. Never! This is chicanery of the lowest order. This is the stock-in-trade of the confidence trickster—a card-sharper! (*He puts them in a cash-box on his desk.*)

NORA. I'm sorry, Roger.

ROGER. Very well. We'll not refer to the subject again. Especially tonight of all nights. Let's forget it. (*He returns to his pipe.*) And I do not wish you to play cards. It is forbidden. Understand?

NORA (*crushed*). I understand, Roger. (*She goes sadly to the window.*)

ROGER. Thank you. (*He puffs his pipe with back to fire.*) Is it still snowing?

NORA (*at the window*). Yes. It's all white outside. And very silent. It makes me feel that you and I are alone in the world.

ROGER. Would you like that?

NORA (*sitting beside him*). Very much.

ROGER. A pleasant fantasy. Might arouse criticism.

NORA. Who would criticise me? We should be alone.

ROGER. Lucinda would be there.

NORA. I should put her out in the snow.

ROGER. An unseasonable and un-Christian thought. (*He returns to his chair.*) By the way, I've only a little gimcrack to put in your stocking. I suppose you do still hang up your stocking?

NORA.   Always—every night.

ROGER.   *Every* night?

NORA.   You're always giving me presents. Everything I have is something you've put in my stocking.

ROGER.   I only do my duty for my little girl.

NORA.   I'm not *your* little girl.

ROGER.   Of course you are.

NORA.   No, Roger. I'm not. I'm no one's little girl. Do you think I can't remember?

ROGER.   That is very ancient history.

(*She sits on the floor beside him.*)

NORA.   Sometimes I'm frightened.

ROGER.   Why?

(*She grips his hand.*)

NORA.   Roger—suppose I only exist in your mind. That I'm not a person at all. That I'm nobody.

ROGER.   That's impossible.

NORA.   You told me that a man called Plato said we only existed in other people's minds.

ROGER.   That was Bishop Berkeley.

NORA.   It might be true.

ROGER.   This is hardly the time for metaphysical philosophy.

NORA (*intensely*).   Why not? This is just the sort of night to talk about these things. I mean—about life and death— and who are we? Who am I? And who are you?

ROGER.   Good gracious.

NORA.   I am like something that you have made up in a fairy-tale. A princess. That's what I feel like. The truth is that I'm just a poor creature without a friend—even without a penny. And yet here I am—sitting by a blazing fire—warm and comfortable. Outside the snow is so deep that it's burying the stone walls. I shall wake up in the morning and say how beautiful it is. But suppose I were in it. Wandering and begging for my food. I might have been. Should I think it beautiful then? Do you know, I think I should like to try.

ROGER.   Begging in the snow?

NORA.   I'd be a real person.

ROGER. Heaven forbid that my lessons should drive you out of doors!

NORA. I would snap my finger at Bishop Berkeley and I would say "Look, I'm real, I'm myself!" I want to feel how little that is, and who I really am.

ROGER. Nora! You belong to me.

NORA. No! I want to be my own father's daughter. And my mother's, too. I haven't spoken of them before. You must please let me tonight. You must talk to me about my father. (ROGER *is silent*.) Was he wicked? You never mention his name. He can do no harm, now he's dead, can he? We oughtn't to despise him—forget him altogether? Ought we?

ROGER. No. Perhaps not.

NORA. Then tell me about him.

ROGER. Why go back into the past?

NORA. Was it something dreadful he did?

ROGER. He took his own life.

NORA. I can remember that. Why were you there, Roger?

ROGER. I was visiting that small hotel in New York. People stay there because it's convenient for the docks. I was saying goodbye to a friend.

NORA. I can remember that hotel. (*She looks into fire*.) There were some palms and a big staircase.

ROGER. Quite right.

NORA. If ever I go back to New York I shall go and look for it.

ROGER. Why?

NORA. Because it's the only home I can remember. (*She turns to him again*.) Tell me—wasn't he wonderfully handsome?

ROGER. I suppose he was.

NORA. He used to play the piano and there was a great deal of singing. My mother used to sing, I'm sure. I can't remember her.

ROGER. I know nothing whatever about her. Except that she is dead. That I do know. They are both dead.

NORA. Poor dead things! Well, so much for the past. Thank you for talking about it, Roger. Do you know, girls at school were always talking about their homes, and their fathers and their mothers. They seemed so much more real than I did.

ROGER. What did they say?

NORA. Oh, you'd be surprised how girls talk, Roger. I never used to say very much. (*She moves behind him.*) My future is fixed. With you. Isn't it? (*She puts her hands on his shoulders.*) Roger—you shall never repent. I shall learn everything you order me to learn. I shall be everything you want me to be. (*She kisses him gravely. He puts his arms to hold her, but drops them as she turns away and goes to the mirror on the piano.*) Oh, how I wish I were pretty!

ROGER (*much disturbed*). You will do well enough as you are, Nora.

NORA. If you're satisfied, I suppose I am. It looks hopeless to me.

(*A knock and* LUCINDA *enters with a lamp.*)

LUCINDA. I brought this. You're all in the dark.

ROGER. Thank you, Lucinda.

LUCINDA (*putting lamp on piano*). It's time the young lady was going to bed?

NORA. No, Lucinda. It's Christmas Eve. And Cousin Hubert hasn't arrived yet.

LUCINDA. From the look of the weather I don't think he'll start, never mind arrive.

ROGER. It's quite heavy.

LUCINDA. Come on.

NORA. Please can't I stay up, tonight?

ROGER. Just a bit longer, Lucinda.

LUCINDA. Very well. Have it your own way. It's ruination.

NORA. I'm not a child any more, am I?

LUCINDA. No, you're not. That's why you ought to go to bed. (NORA *begs with her hands—praying.*) Oh, very well! Ten minutes.

NORA. Thank you!

(LUCINDA *goes.*)

NORA (*sitting on the floor*). Ten minutes. We must make the most of them. Roger . . . ?

ROGER. Yes?

NORA. Has it never struck you as very strange that we should be living together in this way?

ROGER (*looking sharply*). Well . . . not *especially* strange.

NORA. Surely it is! Very strange. What are you? Neither

my brother, nor my father, nor my uncle, nor my cousin—
nor even, by law, my guardian. Roger, is there some secret
in all you've done for me?

ROGER.   Secret?

NORA.   If only you were my long-lost brother!

ROGER.   No!

NORA.   What a pity! (*Rises to tidy fallen leaves, etc., on
her knees.*) I should like that.

ROGER.   Nora, do you never think about the future—the
real future—four or five years hence?

NORA.   A great deal.

ROGER.   What do you think?

NORA.   Promise not to laugh? (*He nods.*) I think about
my husband.

ROGER.   Ah, yes. Well, you'll have a proposal some day.

NORA.   I suppose I shall. I imagine him tall and handsome . . .

ROGER.   Very appropriate.

NORA.   Well educated.

ROGER (*pleased*).   Naturally . . .

NORA.   Clean-shaven.

ROGER (*touching upper lip*).   Of course . . . (*He laughs
complacently.*) What shall you answer?

NORA.   I shall refuse him.

(*She goes to throw rubbish in waste-paper basket.*)

ROGER.   Refuse him?

NORA.   One always refuses an offer of marriage. The first
time anyway. It's one of the rules.

ROGER.   The rules?

NORA.   That's what the girls say at school. But, you know,
Roger, I often try to think of a suitable wife for you. Why
don't you marry?

ROGER.   I hope to. One of these days.

NORA.   I wish you'd do it now. Of course I shall be here
to look after you. Would Mrs. Keith do? She likes you very
much.

ROGER.   How do you know?

NORA.   A woman always knows. Do you like her?

ROGER.   I care for no one—I shall never care for anyone
—but you, Nora.

NORA. Do you mean you care for me so much that you will never marry?

(*He goes to fireplace and takes off smoking cap.*)

ROGER. Ah, Nora, sometimes you are very painful.

NORA (*deeply dramatic*). Very well, Roger. If you don't wish it, I promise never, never, never to marry. I shall be yours alone . . . yours alone!

ROGER. Now don't be theatrical. Ever since Hubert took you to the theatre you've been acting melodrama.

NORA (*running to him and embracing him*). Oh, Roger, I do love you so! I promise never to leave you.

ROGER (*resisting*). No, no! No, Nora, no . . . don't do that! In future I have decided it would be better if you were to limit yourself to one kiss a day.

NORA. Why?

ROGER. You don't understand.

NORA. Are you angry with me?

(*The doorbell rings.*)

ROGER. There. The bell. That will be Hubert.

NORA. I may stay up, mayn't I?

ROGER. I think you had better go to bed.

NORA. Roger? Have I hurt you in some way?

ROGER (*moving away from her*). No. I don't want to hurt *you*. That is all.

NORA. There is some secret. Something you haven't told me. What is it?

(*Voices can be heard in the hall.*)

ROGER. There's Hubert. You'd better go and meet him.

NORA. Dear Hubert! And of course—dear Roger! I do love you both equally, you know. I hope there won't be any jealousy.

ROGER. No. I'm not jealous of my cousin.

(LUCINDA *appears.*)

LUCINDA. It's Mr. Hubert, sir.

(HUBERT *is removing overcoat and overshoes and stamping his feet in the hall.*)

HUBERT. Oh, ho, what a night, what a night!

ROGER. Come in, Hubert, come in. Come to the fire.

NORA. Hello, Cousin!

HUBERT. Hello, my dear! Just let me take these off.

LUCINDA. Come on, miss. Ten minutes. It's over now.

NORA. No! Just when Cousin Hubert arrives! It's not fair. Oh, very well. May I come in later and say goodnight? Please, Roger?

ROGER. Just say goodnight.

LUCINDA. All right, have it your own way. It's ruination! Ruination! And you'll regret it. Come along with you.

(LUCINDA *goes.* NORA *goes to follow.*)

NORA. See you soon.

(HUBERT, *entering, aims a whack at* NORA *as she passes.*)

HUBERT. Off to bed with you! Go on when you're told. I'll be after you.

(*She screams and runs, and* HUBERT *closes the door.*)

ROGER. Come in, Hubert. I'm glad to see you.

HUBERT. Terrible night! Snowing very hard. I had the greatest difficulty making my way.

ROGER. Come over to the fire.

HUBERT (*crossing to fire*). Are you expecting anyone else?

ROGER. No, why?

HUBERT. I wondered. We passed a fellow walking along the road.

ROGER. Will you have a little brandy?

HUBERT. Thank you. My word! That child looks more grown up every time I see her.

(ROGER *pours out brandy.*)

ROGER. Yes. She is a source of great trouble to me.

HUBERT. Why? What's the matter? Is she a naughty child? More than you bargained for?

ROGER. No! I've been longing to see you, Hubert. To see someone—to talk, to get some advice, some sympathy.

HUBERT. Has she developed low tastes? Your very good health.

ROGER. Good health. No, none of those things. Nothing like that, Hubert.

HUBERT. You can always give her a thousand dollars and send her back to her family.

ROGER. Family? She has no family. She's the loneliest as well as the sweetest, and the wisest, and the best of creatures.

(*Cross behind* C *table.*)

HUBERT. Really?

ROGER. Since I began to teach her lessons, in the last few weeks, I have discovered what a wonderful child she is.

HUBERT. Is that so?

ROGER. You'll see. She has grace and charm and deep understanding. She is a natural born philosopher—a keen mathematician — her knowledge of literature positively astounds me.

HUBERT. You astound me also.

ROGER. I couldn't think of parting with her—not for all I possess.

HUBERT. Roger! You talk like a man in love.

ROGER. Yes, I am in love.

HUBERT. Good heavens! (C.)

ROGER. You think it's terrible?

HUBERT. No, no! It's very convenient. If you intend to marry her it could be very helpful.

ROGER. I do intend to marry her.

HUBERT. Good God!

ROGER. I have no reason to be ashamed.

HUBERT. If you have nothing to be ashamed of——

ROGER. Of course not! My ultimate intention is that she should become my wife.

HUBERT. Does she know this?

ROGER. Certainly not!

HUBERT. Why don't you tell her?

ROGER. How can I at my age decently become engaged to a girl of sixteen?

HUBERT. She'll grow up.

ROGER. So shall I! I mean there'll always be a gap between us.

HUBERT. My dear fellow, you take it too hard. (*Puts brandy down on table* C *and lights cigar.*)

ROGER. I take it very seriously. I tell you, it worries me. (*Crosses down* R.) I'm not sleeping very well. I fret about the girl. I keep wondering if I am doing the right thing. I mean, was it right of me to teach her metaphysical philosophy?

HUBERT.   Don't give the girl ideas. Marry her! Now! At once.

ROGER.   Now?

HUBERT.   At once!

ROGER.   It's not so simple as that. Surely you understand —as a man of delicacy?

HUBERT.   You mean she's too young?

ROGER.   Of course.

HUBERT.   Nonsense! A young woman of sixteen married only last week here in Boston. Down South the age of consent is now fourteen. If you're sure of her, the younger the better.

ROGER (*comes* C).   I have a conscience.

HUBERT.   What does your conscience tell you?

ROGER.   I wish to leave her free.

HUBERT.   For what?

ROGER.   To make up her own mind.

HUBERT.   You take a risk. (*Crosses to* ROGER.) A very big risk. She may prefer someone else.

ROGER.   Then I take the risk. I wish to be loved for myself. As other men are loved. What the devil are you laughing at?

HUBERT.   I once made you a promise, Roger. That I should stop you making a fool of yourself.

ROGER (*angry*).   So you think I'm making a fool of myself, do you?

HUBERT.   Not yet. But you're in grave danger. Tell me, what business has a lover with a conscience? It seems to me that if you waste any more time hair-splitting, you'll find your young lady has taken affairs into her own hands, and found somebody else.

ROGER.   Do you think so?

HUBERT.   I'm sure of it.

ROGER.   But she's only a child.

HUBERT.   Is she only a child? If you knew as much about young women as I do, Roger, you'd know they are strangely complicated with thoughts they hardly know themselves. Thoughts that are as old as the world. Take care!

(*A knock on the door.*)

ROGER.   Yes? Who's that? Come in.

(NORA *enters. She wears " a merino dressing-gown, her hair*

*gathered for the night in a single massive coil, loosened by
running". In her hand is a watch.*)

NORA. Am I interrupting you?

ROGER. No. It's all right.

NORA (*crosses D R of* ROGER). Roger, what do you think?
I've lost my watch-key.

ROGER. Again?

NORA. It has most mysteriously disappeared.

ROGER. It did that last time. (*Crosses to desk below her.*)
All your watch-keys seem mysteriously to disappear. (*Turns.*)
Good heavens, look! No slippers!

NORA. I'm sorry. Now Cousin Hubert can really see that
I don't have *les pieds énormes. Nor les mains grosses.* (*She
chatters a phrase or two in French.*) *Je ne suis pas formidable, monsieur* . . .

HUBERT (*playing up*). *Ah, je suis enchanté de vous voir,
mademoiselle, si belle, si élégante!*

NORA. *Merci, monsieur, merci!*

(*There is bowing and by-play between them and* ROGER *is
trying to interrupt.*)

ROGER (*irritated*). Nora! Nora!

NORA (*to* HUBERT). *Excusez-moi, monsieur!*

HUBERT. *Certainement, ma chérie!*

ROGER. You'll get a splinter in your foot or something—
going without slippers. Here's my watch-key.

NORA (*taking it*). Thank you. (*To* HUBERT.) The key!
The key! I have the key . . . !

HUBERT. Who is this charming creature with the beautiful
hands and feet? With the ravishing hair? Surely this is the
face that launched a thousand ships and burned the topless
towers of Ilium?

NORA (*histrionic*). You wrong me, Mr. Maltravers. I am
not she whom you think I am. I am another.

HUBERT. What? Not another?

NORA. Yes, another! Goodbye—for ever!

(*She makes "an exit" behind a pillar U C.* HUBERT *applauds.*)

HUBERT. Bravo! There's acting for you, Roger. That's
what comes of going to the theatre.

NORA (*crossing C*). When can we go to another matinée?

HUBERT. Whenever you say.

ROGER (*ignoring them*).   Does that watch-key fit?

NORA.   No, I'm sorry, Roger, it doesn't fit.

(*She gives back the key.*)

ROGER.   Then you'll have to go to bed.

HUBERT.   Wait a minute.   I have a watch-key, on my chain.

NORA.   Let me try.

HUBERT.   I'll have to take it off.

NORA.   No, no—I'll manage.   Sit down.   (*He sits in arm-chair* L.)   Do you mind if I sit on your knee?

HUBERT.   Not at all.

NORA (*sitting on his knee very delicately*).   Am I too heavy?

HUBERT.   I can manage.

NORA.   There it is.   It works splendidly.   What is the right time, please?

HUBERT (*showing his watch*).   There you are.

NORA.   Good heavens!   Don't tell Roger.   There.   (*She adjusts her watch.*)   I'm so glad to have it going again. Without my watch I should oversleep myself.   Then I should be late for breakfast.

HUBERT.   What would Roger say?

NORA.   He has a terrible bad temper in the morning.

HUBERT.   What a dreadful reputation!

(*They giggle and whisper together.*)

ROGER (*snapping his fingers*).   Nora!   (*He motions her off* HUBERT'S *knee.*)   You're rather big to sit on people's knees now.

NORA (*rising quickly*).   Am I?   I'm sorry, Hubert.

ROGER.   Say goodnight.

NORA.   Goodnight.

HUBERT.   Goodnight, my dear.

(*She kisses* HUBERT *and goes* U C.)

NORA.   Thank you for the key.   Goodnight, Roger.   I'm sorry about my hair.

ROGER.   Nora!

NORA (*turning*).   Yes, Roger?

ROGER. As you have kissed Cousin Hubert, you may also kiss me.

NORA. Thank you. (*She kisses him and goes to the door.*) Goodnight, dear Roger. I hope you two won't quarrel. (*Slowly closing door to frame her face.*) *Bon soir, Monsieur de Rochefaucauld, je t'assure de mes sentiments les plus distinguées.* Oops!

(NORA *goes with a final squeak.*)

HUBERT (*laughing*). There's a handful for you. (*Sits* L.) I can see it's no case for shilly-shallying. You'll have to be strong, decisive.

ROGER (*takes globe to desk*). I wish you wouldn't flirt with the child.

HUBERT. I? Flirt?

ROGER. And I don't want her to go to the theatre again.

HUBERT. You gave us the tickets.

ROGER. It might awaken some inherited tendency to dissipation. All those histrionics.

HUBERT. Nonsense! It was only innocent fun.

ROGER. Don't be a hypocrite. You know perfectly well you find her very attractive.

HUBERT. Of course I do.

ROGER. You do?

HUBERT. I could marry her myself. She's enchanting. I recommend you to marry the young lady and have done with it, before someone else snatches her from you.

ROGER. Not now?

HUBERT. Don't wait too long.

ROGER. I want a responsible, intelligent woman. With freedom of choice.

HUBERT. Here's my advice. Don't sow for others to reap. If you think the harvest isn't ripe enough, let it ripen in milder sunbeams than yours. You'll scorch the girl up. She needs gentle flirtations.

ROGER. Not with you! (*Putting books away.*)

HUBERT. Be realistic—like the French. If you won't marry her now, you should go away. Yes. (*Rises to* C.) Go to Europe. Keep out of the way. Leave her here. Lodge her with some proper person——

ROGER. Yourself, I suppose!

HUBERT. I mean with some good woman. Then in a year's

time come home from Paris, with her trousseau in your trunks, and marry her. And I shall ask no other fee for my advice than the prospect of having an adorable cousin. And some more of this excellent brandy. (*Offers glass.*)

ROGER. I *could* shut her in a convent, I suppose. (*Takes glass.*)

HUBERT. Much to be said for convents. (*He crosses to fire.*)

ROGER. But then she would be childish and stupid.

HUBERT. And contented.

ROGER. The price is too great to pay! No, I shall keep her here.

(NORA *bursts in at the door.*)

NORA. Roger!

ROGER. What is it?

NORA. We have a visitor!

ROGER. Who?

NORA. It's a man!

ROGER. A man? Where?

NORA. Now, please, Roger, don't be angry. Because I think he's very nice. Lucinda has been very rude to him.

ROGER. Who is this fellow?

NORA. He says he's my cousin. My *real* cousin.

ROGER. What are you talking about? You have no cousins —no relations—nobody!

NORA. He says his name is George Fenton.

(LUCINDA *enters.*)

ROGER. I've never heard of him. Who is it, Lucinda?

LUCINDA. I couldn't help it, sir. Really I couldn't. I saw a figure outside the window, so I went to the door . . .

ROGER. Why did you let him in, whoever he is?

LUCINDA. He put his foot in the door and I couldn't close it.

(*There is a knock.*)

NORA. Here he is!

LUCINDA (*scared*). Oh, Mr. Hubert! (*Goes behind table* L C.)

HUBERT. That's all right.

(GEORGE FENTON *enters. A tall lean young man with a south-*

western accent. [*" A man of twenty worlds."*] *He swaggers nonchalantly forward—keen dark eye roving quickly.*)

ROGER. Who are you?

GEORGE. Are you Mr. Lawrence?

ROGER. I am.

GEORGE. The name is Fenton. George Fenton.

ROGER. I don't know you.

GEORGE. No.

ROGER. What are you doing here, then? This is my house.

GEORGE. I'm interested, mister.

ROGER. In what?

GEORGE. I understand you have adopted my cousin.

ROGER. I have a ward, yes. What do you know about her?

GEORGE. Name of Lambert? Nora Lambert?

NORA (*eager*). That's my name.

ROGER (*preventing her shaking hands*). How do I know you're her cousin? What right have you to come forcing your way into my house? Who the devil are you?

GEORGE. I've told you. I'm interested. Perhaps it's time someone took an interest in what's going on round here.

LUCINDA. 'Tis the police will do that!

HUBERT. Hush, Lucinda! (*Comes down* L.) I think this is the fellow I passed on the road.

ROGER. Will you please be good enough to tell me who you are? Or else you're going to go out of here quicker than you came in.

GEORGE (*mocking*). Not out into the snow, I trust, sir?

ROGER. Yes, sir!

GEORGE (*in mock fear*). Oh, no, kind sir! I had hopes of a night's shelter. New York is a long way from here.

NORA (*clutching* ROGER). Please, don't turn him out——

ROGER. Be quiet, Nora!

HUBERT. You're very rude, you know. This is a private house.

GEORGE. Very well, I apologise for the manner of my entrance. I couldn't find any doorbell. And when this old woman tried to push me out I was annoyed.

LUCINDA. Did you hear that, sir?

ROGER. Quiet!

GEORGE. I beg your pardon. I'm from St. Louis, sir. If

I'm not mistaken I'm a relative of this young lady. I knew her father. In fact he was a kind of uncle to me. He was my father's half-brother. We heard of his death, but we never heard what happened to the girl.

NORA. Isn't he some kind of relation?

HUBERT. A half-cousin only.

NORA. But he's mine. A real half-cousin!

GEORGE. You have the right feeling, miss. In the West we say blood is blood, and a cousin is a cousin. And it don't much matter how far removed.

ROGER. I don't know, sir, whether you are an honest man or a scamp. At a venture I suppose I must invite you to stay.

GEORGE. Thank you.

ROGER. Overnight. All right, Lucinda, you see to it, please. Will you be seated, sir?

GEORGE. Thank you.

(GEORGE *takes off his coat and throws it to* LUCINDA.)

LUCINDA (*firmly*). Miss Nora!

NORA (*to* ROGER). Please—not yet!

ROGER. Let her stay. I may need her. I have some questions to ask.

(LUCINDA *goes*.)

GEORGE (*warming his hands*). This is a nice place. It's better here than outside.

NORA. The poor man's cold!

(*She pushes* HUBERT *away from fire and then sits down* L.)

HUBERT (*holding up decanter*). May I suggest?

ROGER. Very well.

HUBERT. Would you care to have a little of this?

GEORGE. Well, thank you, now you mention it. After all, it is Christmas Eve. You all look very quiet and sober for Christmas.

ROGER. We are quiet and sober people, Mr. . . . I didn't catch your name.

GEORGE. Fenton. George Fenton. Thank you. Your good health. Especially to you, pretty cousin. And a merry Christmas to all. Thank you.

(*He passes back the glass, expecting more.* HUBERT *refills it.*)

GEORGE. You're younger than I thought you would be, Mr. Lawrence.

ROGER. Indeed?

GEORGE. I expected an old gentleman. The sort who adopts children to comfort his old age.

ROGER. I'm sorry I disappoint you.

NORA. Please—do you remember my father well?

GEORGE. Very well.

NORA. What was he like?

GEORGE. Very handsome. I'm supposed to take after him.

NORA. Really?

GEORGE. I knew your mother, too.

NORA. Oh, did you . . . ? Tell me.

GEORGE. She was very beautiful.

NORA. Was she?

GEORGE. Don't you remember St. Louis? No, you were only a little girl. I'll tell you one thing. There was always singing in your house. Your mother was a happy kind of person. She'd lead off the singing. And there we were, all of us, roaring our heads off, fit to bust the roof.

(HUBERT *refills* GEORGE'S *glass*.)

ROGER. The sort of thing that happens in many houses in St. Louis.

GEORGE. Sure. We're happy people down there.

ROGER. Can you tell us nothing more precise?

NORA. But I do remember singing. I can always hear singing.

GEORGE. You hold on to that. It's a good thing to remember.

HUBERT (*giving glass to* GEORGE). You are still on trial, Mr. Fenton. Have you no other corroborative details?

GEORGE. Any other what?

NORA. Cousin Hubert is a lawyer. He wants facts.

GEORGE. I see. What do you want me to say? That her father gambled his money? That her mother ran away?

NORA. What did he say?

ROGER. Nothing.

NORA. About my mother? What else is there?

GEORGE. Only that I know she was a very kind lady. And a very brave one. We heard she had died. It was in a fire—in a theatre somewhere.

ROGER. An actress?

GEORGE. That is correct.

ROGER. That is quite enough!

GEORGE. Look, I didn't come here to make you sad. This is Christmas. (*To* HUBERT.) Thank you. I don't know your name, but I don't mind if I do.

(*He gives* HUBERT *his glass.*)

ROGER. That is my cousin, Mr. Hubert Lawrence. And I wish you wouldn't drink all my brandy.

GEORGE. Another cousin? All one big happy family. How do you do, sir? (*Taking drink.*) Glad to meet you.

HUBERT. I wouldn't advise too much on an empty stomach.

NORA. May I get Mr. Fenton something to eat?

ROGER. Anything you like.

GEORGE. So I'm now accepted into the bosom of the family.

ROGER. No, sir. You are given shelter for the night. That's all.

NORA. I'll get you something.

GEORGE. Thank you, little cousin.

HUBERT. I'll help you.

ROGER. No, no, Hubert . . .

(HUBERT *goes out with* NORA. GEORGE *and* ROGER *are left, alone.* ROGER *gestures helplessly to* HUBERT *as he goes.* GEORGE *takes another drink, whistling softly. Then he goes and sits at the piano, playing the tune—" Holy Night "— with one finger.*)

GEORGE. You don't trust me, do you, Mr. Lawrence?

ROGER. I suspend judgement.

GEORGE. Ho, ho! Wise old bird! What are you afraid of?

ROGER. I am quite indifferent to you, sir. I think it unfortunate that you should come here, and drag up Nora's past.

GEORGE. She seems delighted to have a past.

ROGER. All that is forgotten.

GEORGE. Anyway, she claims me for her own.

ROGER. A very slight relationship, Mr. Fenton.

GEORGE. All the better.

ROGER. Why?

GEORGE. If she fell in love with me there'd be no—what do you call it?—consanguinity.

ROGER. You are offensive, sir!

GEORGE. That hurt you, didn't it?

ROGER. I don't know what you're talking about.

GEORGE. Why don't you take me as a friend—not as an enemy?

ROGER. I don't wish to take you as anything. You have forced your acquaintance upon me.

GEORGE. What do you want to do with that girl, anyway? Eh? What does Nora mean to you exactly? Got some designs, Mr. Lawrence? Eh? There is, in Boston I believe, a thing they call the Watch and Ward Society. They keep an eye on men like you, Mr. Lawrence.

(*He turns to the keyboard and plays a few chords.* ROGER *glowers murderously.* HUBERT *enters as waiter with napkin.* NORA *enters carrying a tray, which she places on piano.* LUCINDA *follows.*)

NORA. I *thought* I could hear music. You play, Mr. Fenton?

GEORGE. I can vamp a tune. Remember your mother singing this?

(*He plays "Camptown Races".* NORA *joins in.* GEORGE *and* HUBERT *join in chorus.* HUBERT *and* NORA *dance together. Even* LUCINDA *sings.* ROGER *can bear no more and strides to the piano.*)

ROGER. Silence! Stop that hideous noise! (*He slams the lid of the piano.*) Nora, go to bed! Go with her, Lucinda.
LUCINDA (*firmly*). Miss Nora!

(NORA *and* LUCINDA *go,* NORA *saying a hesitant goodnight.*)

ROGER. Goodnight. I'll thank you to remember what night this is, Mr. Fenton. And also whose house you are in. Mr. Lawrence will no doubt be willing to see to your needs. I hope they are not too offensive. Goodnight!

(ROGER *goes.* GEORGE *looks at* HUBERT *in amazement and whistles.* HUBERT *gives him the napkin. He attacks the food. He is at the piano still.*)

GEORGE. Ah! This is real hospitality. (*He holds out his empty glass to* HUBERT.) Would you mind?

(HUBERT *takes it and pours brandy at table* C. GEORGE *plays "God rest you merry gentlemen" with one finger.*)

CURTAIN

END OF ACT TWO, SCENE ONE

ACT II

SCENE 2

Early New Year. The snow is still lying outside.

There is bright morning sunshine. LUCINDA *opens the door.*
ISABEL *enters, dressed for driving. She goes over to the fire,*
as it is cold.

ISABEL. Thank you, Lucinda. I called on my way into
town. Is Nora here?
LUCINDA. She's outside, walking, with the young man.
ISABEL. Is he still here?
LUCINDA. He is. There's some people would outstay their
welcome even if you was to put them on an iceberg.

(ROGER *enters.*)

ROGER. Good morning, Isabel. This is a pleasant surprise.
Are you well?
ISABEL. Yes, thank you.
ROGER (*to* LUCINDA). Tell Mr. Fenton the sleigh is calling
for him at half-past nine.
LUCINDA. I will, sir. I'll call him. He's out there disporting
himself.
ISABEL. Would Nora like to come shopping with me?
ROGER. No, thank you. Not this morning. Thank you,
Isabel. The holiday is over. (LUCINDA *goes.* ROGER *goes to*
the window.) I wonder what on earth those two find to talk
about. Look at him, lounging along with Nora, with a cigar
in his mouth. One of mine, too! Doesn't even take it out
when he speaks to her.
ISABEL. Remember, Roger, nothing succeeds with a woman
like just too little deference.
ROGER. Deference? He's positively uncouth with her.
Anyway, he leaves this morning.

ISABEL. I think you have been very patient to let him stay so long.

ROGER. Ten days is a long time with Master Fenton in the house. Snowed up.

ISABEL. Such terrible weather! I haven't been able to leave the house either. All the same, you should have kept them apart.

ROGER. What am I to do? He *is* her cousin.

ISABEL. And a link with her past. That's why she likes him so much.

ROGER. Have you noticed the fellow has a tattoo mark—there—on his left wrist?

ISABEL. He's a kinsman, and a godsend. Tattooed or untattooed. I do sympathise with the girl. She has known so few young men.

ROGER. I have taught her, I hope, how to recognise a gentleman.

ISABEL. Gentlemen may not be what her instinct requires, Roger. Not at that age. She has not yet learned to be fastidious in her choice.

ROGER. He is what is called "a man of the world", I suppose?

ISABEL. A man of twenty worlds, I should say.

ROGER. Anyway, he goes. This morning.

ISABEL (*crossing* L). Roger, I have something important to tell you. I sail for Europe on the fifteenth of next month. I have booked my passage.

ROGER. So soon?

ISABEL. I have booked a passage also for one other person.

ROGER. Who is that?

ISABEL. Nora. I want to take her with me.

ROGER. That's impossible.

ISABEL. Let me take her to Europe for a season and bring her out in Rome. Don't be afraid. I will guard her as if she were my own. Indeed, Roger—I sometimes wish she were.

ROGER. You wish . . . Isabel? This is very kind of you. Very kind indeed . . . but I can't allow it.

ISABEL. Why not?

ROGER. I must complete her education.

ISABEL. I will teach her to be fastidious.

ROGER. I beg your pardon?

ISABEL. I will make her able to distinguish between one

man and another. In Europe she will learn to be a European. Some of that " culture of the centuries " may rub off on to her. She will learn to know the best—and to make the best of herself.

ROGER. I suppose you want to take her away from me!

ISABEL. The time will soon pass.

ROGER. Do you want to deprive me of everything? Even this new idea—this great dream of my life—to create a perfect wife for myself. Do you want to deprive me of that?

ISABEL. No. Roger. I will make your dream a reality.

ROGER. If you take her away I shall lose her.

ISABEL. How?

ROGER. She'll meet someone better. Or become so fastidious she will have nothing to do with me at all.

ISABEL. I give you my word to bring her back to you.

ROGER. No! (*He turns away.*)

ISABEL. You are afraid to take the chance—of giving her her freedom?

ROGER. I have given her all the freedom she needs.

ISABEL. Roger—you fathead!

ROGER. Isabel—that is not polite!

ISABEL. Oh, but you are! You're in love with an idea. Don't think this fashioning of a wife to order is going to give you happiness. As though she were some bloom in a hothouse. Oh, Roger, I could kick you. There's a fatuous sort of long-winded patience about you—the lofty arrogance of a rich young man. Take care Mr. Fenton doesn't throw a brick through your hothouse window.

ROGER. Fenton?

ISABEL. The young man is after adventure. He's on the make. He comes to make love to his cousin, and marry her if he can.

ROGER. I trust Nora to keep her friendship within the bounds of cousinship.

ISABEL. Very well. If you won't let me help you.

ROGER. Thank you—no.

ISABEL. I must go then. The offer is open. Goodbye. (*She goes towards the door.*)

ROGER. I'll see you to the door.

ISABEL (*a parting shot*). And remember, Roger, people are beginning to gossip.

ROGER. About what?

ISABEL. About you and a young girl.
ROGER. Damnable impertinence.
ISABEL. What else did you expect? You stupid fellow!

(ISABEL *goes. He follows.*)

ROGER (*expostulating*). But, Isabel . . . What senseless gossip is this? Nora is far too young to think of any attachment. She's still a child . . .

(NORA *and* GEORGE *can be heard laughing outside. They appear in the window.* NORA *runs into the room.*)

NORA. No, no. I've no breath left. No, you brute! You mustn't throw snowballs in here. Lucinda wouldn't like it.
GEORGE (*entering, wiping his hands*). Lucinda sounded very glad to be rid of me.
NORA. Your train's at ten o'clock.

(NORA *closes the hall door.*)

GEORGE. I suppose that's the end.
NORA. Oh, dear!
GEORGE. Are you sorry?
NORA (*taking off her coat and hat*). Mmm . . .
GEORGE. You don't sound it.
NORA. Oh, I am.

(GEORGE *picks up his valise and puts it on the table.*)

GEORGE. I'm all packed, anyway. My few belongings are here.
NORA (*going to her work-basket*). Wait a minute. I have a present for you. (*She takes out a pair of slippers.*)
GEORGE. My! Those are fine!
NORA. I just have to finish the sewing.
GEORGE. Fancy you doing these for me!

(*He puts an arm round her. She moves away, to chair* C.)

NORA. Please! I must finish this before Roger comes. I have to start lessons again.
GEORGE. What on earth does he find to teach you about?
NORA. A great many things.
GEORGE (*closing in*). I could teach you more.
NORA. Behave yourself.

GEORGE. What an extraordinary man he is.

NORA. Why?

GEORGE. Imagine me adopting a little girl.

NORA. You and Roger are very different types.

GEORGE. Thank God! What does he expect to do with you?

NORA. He has made me what I am.

GEORGE (*patting and admiring her*). I don't think he had much to do with it.

NORA. What would have happened to me?

GEORGE. You'd have managed. With a figure like that. (*He crosses to desk.*) Does he expect to educate you forever? (*He picks up a notebook.*) What's this? Patagonia! Ha! (*He gives a derisive laugh.*)

NORA. Put that down.

GEORGE. You seem to me to have all the learning a pretty woman needs. You ought to come out West and see your own people. You're a regular Western girl.

NORA. Do you think so?

GEORGE. Out West is the only place for a man of ideas. Round here you're all stuck fast in ten feet of varnish.

NORA. Am I?

GEORGE. I'll pull you out of it! Comes of living with a stiff-necked blue-nosed Bostonian . . .

NORA. Please understand—once and for all—that I refuse to listen to disrespectful remarks about Roger!

GEORGE (*mimicking*). Oh, bow-wow, Miss Boston!

NORA. I mean it!

GEORGE. You're splendid when you look like that.

NORA. Be sensible!

GEORGE. All I have to do is attack your papa.

NORA. He is not my papa.

GEORGE. What is he, then? Are you going to marry him?

NORA. Marry Roger!

GEORGE. That's what he's up to.

NORA. How could you say that?

GEORGE. He's a man, isn't he? Or isn't he?

NORA. I shall do what Roger wishes.

GEORGE. Roger be hanged! You're not his slave! You must choose for yourself—act for yourself.

NORA. I have no right. I belong to him.

GEORGE. Belong! (*He rises.*) You must obey your own

heart. You don't know what you're talking about. One of these days your heart will have its say. Don't tell me seriously that you could ever love a solemn old fop like that!

NORA (*rising and going to work-basket*). You have no right . . . to speak of Roger in that way.

GEORGE. Don't protest, dear girl. I must have my say. I speak in your own interest. From my own heart. I detest the man. I came here perfectly on the square—and he's treated me as if I weren't fit to touch with tongs. I know I'm poor. I have my way to make. I ain't fashionable. But for all that, take me altogether, I'm as good as he is. Why can't he be frank—take me by the hand and say, " Come, my friend, I've got capital, and you've got brains. Let's pull together." Does he think I want to steal his spoons or pick his pocket? Is that Bostonian hospitality? It's a poor kind if it is.

NORA. I wish you and he could be friends.

GEORGE. Friends! He'd gladly stick a knife in my back.

NORA. You are the two men I care for most in the world.

GEORGE. You do care for me, don't you?

NORA. I've told you.

GEORGE (*taking her hands*). Choose, then—choose! Choose between me and him.

NORA. Can't you see how difficult it is?

GEORGE (*holding her*). Nothing's difficult. (*He kisses her very slowly and gently.*) See. That was easy, wasn't it? I'll give you my address in New York. When you can get away —you come to me. I'll look after you. Then you can choose —for yourself.

NORA (*breaking away*). No! . . .

GEORGE. Very well, then, I'm afraid you'll have to give me up. I wish I'd never seen you. Making me fall in love with you. Are those my slippers? (*He takes them to his valise.*)

NORA (*stunned*). Yes . . .

GEORGE. They're very nice slippers. (*He pops slippers in valise.*) Thank you very much. Something to remember you by. Well, I must be off. I suppose I'm in the way.

NORA (*going to him*). Do you really wish you'd never seen me?

GEORGE. No, not really. I suppose it was worth it. Look, if you're ever in New York, that's my address. Franks and Fenton, Scrap Iron Merchants. (*He gives her a card.*)

NORA. Is that what you do?

GEORGE. Yes. And not much in it, I can tell you. You can't get far without capital.

NORA. And you haven't any?

GEORGE. My dear girl, I'm a poor man!

NORA. How poor?

GEORGE. Poor, poor, poor! Poor as a rat. Look there. (*He shows two bills.*) Two dollars. That's my total fortune.

NORA. All you've got in the world?

GEORGE (*singing*).
> " He was poor but he was honest,
>   Victim of the rich man's game . . ."

NORA. George! Is that all?

GEORGE. Afraid so. (NORA *runs to her work-basket and fumbles in it.*) What's it got to do with you?

NORA. I have some money here.

(*She takes out a roll of notes.*)

GEORGE. Now what are you up to?

NORA. Roger lets me have this to give away. Or buy things. Or anything I want. There's eighty dollars here.

(GEORGE *walks away, down* R.)

GEORGE. That's *your* money.

NORA. Roger lets me give what I please to charity——

GEORGE. You call this charity?

NORA. I didn't mean that. Please take them.

GEORGE. Is that all you have?

NORA. Roger will give me more. (*She holds out the notes.*)

(ROGER *walks in.*)

ROGER. It's time Mr. Fenton left for the station. The sleigh is at the door.

NORA (*still holding out the notes*). Please!

ROGER. What's all this?

NORA. Please, George!

ROGER. What are you doing?

GEORGE. I'm afraid I must bid you goodbye.

NORA. George!

ROGER. Please don't insist, Nora. Wait till my back is turned.

NORA. There is nothing to be ashamed of. Is there?

GEORGE. Yes. My poverty. Poverty is shameful.

ROGER. Honest poverty is never shameful.

GEORGE. A great deal you know about it.

ROGER. If you need money, don't appeal to her. Come to me.

NORA. He didn't appeal to me. I appealed to him. He has only two dollars in the world.

ROGER. How do you know?

NORA. He told me.

ROGER. Ah? (GEORGE *turns away in anger to desk*.) Is this true? (ROGER *takes out his pocket-book*.) You must let me help you. It was very stupid of me not to have guessed your embarrassment. (ROGER *counts out bills*.) A man once asked me for a loan of a hundred dollars. I refused him. I am sorry to say with fatal results. Let me put my conscience right.

NORA (*to* GEORGE). Don't be proud. Roger means well.

ROGER. No. Don't be proud, Mr. Fenton. There's a hundred dollars.

(*There is a pause.* GEORGE *goes over and takes them.*)

GEORGE. You win that trick, Mr. Lawrence. But you can take them back. (*He holds* ROGER'S *hand and slams the bills into it.*) Because I'm not giving you the chance to play the bountiful gentleman. Which is a trick to me.

ROGER. You refuse, then?

GEORGE. I reject the insult. Which makes us equal, I think.

ROGER. Very well.

(ROGER *crushes up the notes and throws them on the fire.*)

NORA. Roger!

GEORGE. Ho, ho! He's thrown a hundred dollars on the fire! That's game to me, I think.

NORA. Roger, are you mad?

(*She runs to the fire.*)

GEORGE (*holding her back*). Come back! Don't burn yourself. He has made a mighty gesture. Don't spoil it.

NORA. Please go. You must leave the house. Something dreadful will happen.

GEORGE. Mr. Lawrence will burn down the house, I expect. Rich men feel guilty about great possessions. (*He takes up his valise.*) Well, goodbye. I hope your conscience is easier. What a murky conscience it must be!

(NORA *offers her roll of notes.*)

NORA. Please, take these!

GEORGE (*selects one note*). I'll take that. Just one dollar. I will keep this in remembrance of you, Nora, and only spend it for my last dinner. Goodbye, Mr. Lawrence. And thank you. My hand, I think. Goodbye, Nora. Remember. Any time.

(GEORGE *kisses her on the forehead. Then he goes out.* NORA *runs to the door to follow but stops and presses her head against the door. The front door slams.* NORA *runs to the window.* ROGER *takes up his books for the lesson. The noise of sleigh bells going away.* NORA *is wiping her eyes.*)

RORER. Are you ready?

NORA. Yes . . . I'm ready . . .

ROGER. What's the matter? Are you crying? Because that fellow has gone?

NORA (*weeping*). Yes.

ROGER. So that's how it is!

(NORA *turns from the window.*)

I hope you will soon get over it. You are not likely to meet him again. Take out your books. And take this.

(*He gives her a handkerchief.* NORA *dries her eyes and obeys.* ROGER *finds his notebook.* NORA *carries books to the table.*)

NORA. I'm sorry, Roger. I must be a great disappointment to you.

ROGER. Please don't start again. I have made arrangements for your future. You will be going to Europe with Mrs. Keith. You will sail on the fifteenth of February.

NORA. You are sending me away!

ROGER. It is for your own good. Mrs. Keith has made this generous offer. I have decided to accept it. Dry your eyes. Let us hope for the best. What is it this morning?

NORA (*sitting*). Geography?

ROGER (*turning the pages*).　Where are we?

NORA (*her back to him*).　Patagonia.

ROGER.　I shall ask you ten questions. Are you ready?

NORA.　Yes, I'm ready.

ROGER.　Population?

(NORA *shoots the answers back on the verge of tears.*)

NORA.　Scanty.

ROGER.　Climate?

NORA.　Arid.

ROGER.　Geological formation?

NORA (*with rising indignation*).　Tertiary calciniferous basaltic!

ROGER.　Customs?

NORA (*tearful and furious*).　Beastly!

ROGER.　People?

NORA.　God damn awful!　(*She cries and runs.* ROGER *is shocked.*)

CURTAIN

END OF ACT TWO

ACT III

Scene 1

The same room in Roger's *house, fifteen months later. It is spring and the curtains are the same as at the beginning.*

Isabel *and* Hubert *have just arrived.* Isabel *is unwrapping a box of lilacs and blossom at the table.* Hubert *is at the fireplace.*

Isabel.   I didn't realise he'd been so ill.
Hubert.   He ordered me not to tell you.
Isabel.   I wouldn't have spent all this time in New York if I'd known.
Hubert.   He wanted you to.

(Lucinda *enters with a vase.*)

Isabel.   Thank you, Lucinda. That's just the thing.

(*She continues putting flowers in vase at the piano.*)

Hubert.   What did the doctor say, Lucinda?
Lucinda (c).   The doctor says he's satisfied.
Hubert.   That's a good thing.
Lucinda.   Yes, but I'm not.
Hubert.   Why not?
Lucinda.   He's not eating.
Isabel.   Are you sure it's all right Nora rushing up to see him? Won't she excite him too much?
Lucinda.   Ah, Miss Nora will be like a ministering angel to him.
Hubert.   Hope she doesn't finish him off!
Lucinda.   He's waited so long for her, poor man. I've heard him talking in his fever, crying out her name. All those long weeks, when the stupor was on him, he would be talking about her, and ask me a dozen times if she had arrived, and

forgot as often as I told him—the dear man, who used to remember the very hairs of her head. He kept wondering whether anything had happened to her, and late in the evening, when the carriages began to pass, he cried out that each one of them was herself, and what would she be thinking of him for not coming to meet her. " Don't tell her how bad I am," he says.

HUBERT. Now, Lucinda!

LUCINDA. And then once at midnight, the wind began to blow, and he declared it was a storm, and your ship was on the coast. " God keep her safe!" he cried. Then he asked if she was changed and grown, and was she pretty? (*She picks up mirror from piano.*) And he took the handglass and looked at himself and cried out he was ugly and horrible and she would hate him.

ISABEL. Good gracious! Poor dear Roger!

LUCINDA. And now he's fretting and won't speak to me. Sitting up there in his dressing-gown, looking out of the window. Day after day.

HUBERT. Mightn't the excitement be too much?

ISABEL. Don't let her stay up there too long.

LUCINDA. It's kill or cure, Mrs. Keith. Kill or cure!

HUBERT. Well, you're in charge.

LUCINDA. I am, sir, and a terrible time I've had. I'll just go and see what's happening up there.

(LUCINDA *goes, taking empty flower-box with her.*)

HUBERT (U C). We have to make some allowance for Lucinda's sense of the dramatic. But he was bad, you know. Pneumonia, I think. That's why he sent me to New York to meet you. Anyway, the sight of Nora's going to cheer him up.

ISABEL. I do hope he approves of her. She is, after all, my creation now.

HUBERT. You've done very well. She's so beautiful and so wise.

ISABEL. You must stop flirting with the girl.

HUBERT. I don't!

ISABEL. Oh, yes, you do. I've watched you. Ever since you met us at the gangway in New York you've eyes for no one else.

HUBERT. That is not entirely true. You have grown more beautiful also! If that were possible. . . .

ISABEL. Do you think a young girl is like a piano—to be strummed on for a pretty tune? Leave her alone.

HUBERT. Ought she to be wasted on Roger?

ISABEL. That is not for us to judge. Why didn't you tell me he was so ill?

HUBERT. Strict orders. Nora's pleasure in New York must not be spoiled, he said.

ISABEL. So you made the most of it. I warn you—I have a fierce maternal pride in that girl. I'm proud of her.

HUBERT. She'll be a sensation. And she won't be short of offers.

ISABEL. Don't I know it! She could have had two million-aires in Rome, the nephew of an archduke in Venice, and a variety of English noblemen in Paris. But I kept my bargain. I brought her home for Roger. She is his speculation—his property. Unless he's thought better of it.

HUBERT. I'm afraid not.

ISABEL. He still wants her?

HUBERT (*drawing a legal envelope from his pocket*). As Roger's lawyer I have no right to reveal his affairs. But this is something he wants me to tell you. He has settled this house and half his fortune on Nora.

ISABEL. As a marriage settlement?

HUBERT. Unconditionally. Whether she marries him or not, it doesn't matter. This is to make her independent. To give her perfect freedom of choice.

ISABEL. He has kept his bargain. I must keep mine.

HUBERT. As his lawyer I am bound to carry out his wishes. As his cousin I ought to save him from his folly.

ISABEL. I don't trust you!

HUBERT. He once asked me at all costs to stop him making a fool of himself.

ISABEL. That's no reason why you should make a bigger one of yourself.

HUBERT. It isn't a very good match.

ISABEL. Roger is a very good man.

HUBERT. So good! But virtue was never very entertaining, was it?

ISABEL. Listen to the fashionable New Yorker!

HUBERT. I give you my worldly opinion.

ISABEL. Keep it for your worldly clients and leave my Nora alone. You are quite unsuitable.

HUBERT.　What a worthy opponent you must be in battle!

ISABEL.　Yes, I am! Take care.

HUBERT.　And so loyal to Roger.

ISABEL.　Of course. My duty is to him.

HUBERT.　What a wife you would have made!

ISABEL.　Tush! That's all over.

HUBERT.　Is it? You are a most attractive woman, Mrs. Keith. Especially when the fire blazes in your eyes.

ISABEL (*walking away from him to window*).　Stupid man!

HUBERT (*following her*).　Europe has changed you, too. Wait till Roger sees you.

ISABEL (*bitterly*).　Roger will never notice.

(*There is a knock on the door and* LUCINDA *appears.*)

LUCINDA (*breathless*).　If you please, sir . . . ma'am . . . !

HUBERT.　Yes, Lucinda, what is it?

LUCINDA.　It's Mr. Roger, sir!

ISABEL.　Is he worse?

LUCINDA.　He's coming down!

ISABEL.　What!

HUBERT.　Are you sure that's a good thing?

LUCINDA.　I couldn't stop him. . . . (ROGER *appears. He wears a dressing-gown.*) Are you sure you're feeling all right, sir?

ROGER.　Perfectly all right, thank you. There's nothing the matter with me.

LUCINDA.　But the doctor said——

ROGER.　I don't care what the doctor said. Isabel, dear Isabel! I'm so glad to see you home. Thank you for the beautiful flowers!

ISABEL.　Are you sure you ought to be doing this, Roger?

ROGER.　Of course! The doctor told me to take exercise.

LUCINDA.　But you're not to over-tire yourself, sir.

ROGER.　Go away, Lucinda, you're a silly old woman! Hullo, Hubert!

(*He crosses to* HUBERT, *who shakes his hand.*)

HUBERT.　You've made a splendid recovery.

LUCINDA.　Thank God for the miracle!

(LUCINDA *goes to the door, watching for* NORA.)

ROGER.　Nora is the miracle! What have you done to her?

ISABEL.   I just let her grow up.

ROGER.   She's remarkable!

LUCINDA (*at door*).   She's like an angel in shining raiment. Here she comes!

(NORA *appears in the doorway. It is a breathtaking moment, as she stands there in a dress which* ISABEL *must have chosen and a beam of morning sunshine falls on her.* HUBERT *goes to her and holds out his hand. The ringmaster rises to the occasion.*)

HUBERT.   Aha! What do we see? The American version of Pallas Athene. Born in Missouri. For years she wore aprons and carried lesson books. Then one fine day she was eighteen, in a fine silk dress from Paris. (HUBERT *hands her down the step and over to* ROGER.) Let me present to you— the New American Woman!

NORA (*laughing*).   No, no, no! I'm no different, really. But I'm so happy to be home again. Everything's just the same. Even Roger.

(*But there is a new grace and poise, even if the old* NORA *still peeps through.*)

ROGER (*taking her hands*).   Let me look at you again. I must hear all about your travels. Thank you, Hubert, for bringing them home.

HUBERT.   Thank you for the privilege of escorting two such desirable ladies.

NORA.   Hubert gave us a wonderful time in New York. We've been to theatres and concerts and all kinds of entertainments.

ROGER.   I'm a miserable fool to let myself be laid low at a time like this. Anyway, I'm better now. You have a new hat, Isabel.

ISABEL.   Thank you, Roger. I can take it off now.

HUBERT (*giving legal document to* ROGER).   Here's the deed. You sign there—and there—with a witness. . . .

NORA.   He noticed your hat!

ISABEL.   Yes. He noticed my hat.

(*The gong rings.*)

ROGER (*putting document in pocket*).   There!   That's

Lucinda calling you. You'd better go. I hope you enjoy your luncheon, Isabel.

HUBERT. Hear that! He wants to be rid of us. We take notice, sir. We take notice. Will you come?

(HUBERT *holds out his arm to* ISABEL, *as the gong rings again.*)

ISABEL. Thank you. Don't over-excite him, Nora.

ROGER. I need excitement! (HUBERT *and* ISABEL *go together.*) Now, I want to hear all about it.

NORA. You shall. (*She indicates the armchair and he sits.*) But there's so much to tell. I don't know where to begin.

ROGER (*grandly*). Begin with Rome.

NORA. Rome! Oh, Roger, shall I ever see it again? (*She shuts her eyes.*) I mean in reality. When I close my eyes it's still there. I can see the blue Campagna from our window on the Pincian—and the Piazza di Spagna quite close by—it's a city of miracles, Roger!

ROGER. I should like to see it again.

NORA. And the churches! One for every day of the year —like a new hat. Santa Maria Maggiore—Ara Coeli—Santa Constanza—and of course the great grand old St. Peter's itself.

ROGER. I hope you were not converted.

NORA. Only to worldly vanities. Which I confess I enjoy vastly.

ROGER. I'm glad to hear it.

NORA. If you only knew! (*She twirls happily and lands by his chair.*) The clothes I've brought back—and the trinkets. You sent me so much money. My bank account always seemed full. Oh, Roger, I do thank you.

(*She goes to kiss him.*)

ROGER. Thank you, my dear! No, take care! This germ, whatever it is, may still be lingering. It's my chest.

NORA. I don't mind a bit. I'd like to nurse you.

ROGER. You've cheered me up a lot. Go on.

NORA. Sure I'm not tiring you?

ROGER. Not a bit.

NORA. Did I tell you I came out in Rome?

ROGER. Really?

NORA (*crossing to fire and twirling*). Out, out, out! A thousand miles out—in pink and blue, and every colour of the rainbow.

ROGER. Marvellous.

NORA. It was at the great ball of the Princess Xara. In a palazzo. How the Princess Xara came to invite me I don't know. But she did. Mrs. Keith was like a fairy godmother. She shod me in glass slippers, and to the ball we went. It's all right—I came home with both my slippers on my feet. It was terrifying. I had to curtsey to the princess. She was very condescending. Looking down her nose and said. " Who eez dis? " I looked up, and I thought—if only you knew, my dear Princess, you'd have the footmen throw me out! I'm plain Nora Lambert from St. Louis and nothing's going to alter that. But no one penetrated my disguise. I am now accepted in Roman society. I can drop a curtsey to a condescending princess, or a little bow to a good old cardinal, as smartly as you please. I am now finished. Done to a turn. I hope you like me better.

ROGER. I like you very much.

NORA. I have to confess that I'm hopelessly frivolous. Do you mind? (*Another happy twirl U C.*)

ROGER. A little frivolity is permissible in a woman.

NORA. Not too much.

ROGER. Not too much.

NORA. I'm afraid I have utterly cast away my childhood.

ROGER. That is inevitable.

NORA. I was stupid—diffident. Now I speak up to people as bold as can be.

ROGER. A certain boldness in conversation can be attractive.

NORA. But not too much.

ROGER. Not too much. It is the great fault of our American woman. Avoid it if you can.

NORA. Of course.

ROGER. Of course. (*They laugh.*)

NORA. I've missed you, Roger. So much I wanted to know. All about the emperors and the popes. . . .

(LUCINDA *enters with a tray.*)

LUCINDA. Now, sir, are you ready for your meal? I hope you're not tiring yourself out listening to her stories. Will you bring up a chair, Miss Nora? (NORA *pushes up armchair to table.*) There, that's right. Can you eat that, Mr. Roger?

ROGER. Why shouldn't I eat it?

LUCINDA. Thanks be to God! You've got your appetite back.

ROGER. Lucinda has been starving me.

LUCINDA. Oh, yes! Will you take this, Miss Nora?

NORA. Thank you. This looks delicious. May I start?

ROGER. Please do. Thank you, Lucinda. I think we have everything. No, give Miss Nora some wine. I'll have some, too.

LUCINDA. Do you think the doctor would like it, sir?

ROGER. I don't give that for the doctor.

(*He snaps his fingers.*)

LUCINDA. Indeed? So that's how it is, is it?

ROGER. That's how it is.

LUCINDA. Oh, very well.

(LUCINDA *goes out, meaningful.*)

NORA. You'll have to forgive me, Roger. I have an enormous appetite. I'm afraid I'm going to cost you a great deal of money. May I do this? (*She takes up a leg of chicken.*) In Europe they do this.

ROGER. Do they really?

NORA (*eating*). Yes. The Count of Bel Ferona takes a piece in each hand.

ROGER. Indeed?

NORA. And he talks with his mouth full.

(*She giggles at the thought of him.*)

ROGER (*grave*). I see. The Count of Bel Ferona is, of course, a foreigner.

NORA. Oh, yes, Italian.

ROGER. Of course.

NORA (*laughs*). What fun this is!

ROGER (*watching her*). Is everything to your liking?

NORA. It's wonderful—to be home again!

ROGER. It's wonderful to have you home again.

NORA. Aren't you eating?

ROGER. I take my time.

NORA. I've so much looked forward to this. And now it's true. So beautifully true.

ROGER. You love this house?

NORA. Oh, I do!

ROGER. I hope you won't find it dull after Rome.

NORA. Of course not. Though I don't think anything will ever be the same again after Rome.

ROGER. But you could continue to live here?

NORA. But of course!

ROGER. It's a valuable property, you know. Worth many thousands.

NORA. I'm sure it is.

ROGER. If you were an heiress, and you had a great deal of money at your disposal, would you make many changes?

NORA (*looking round*). I don't think so. I love the old place as it is. Why, Roger?

ROGER. I just wondered.

(LUCINDA *returns with the wine and also a bottle of medicine.* NORA *is puzzled but goes on eating.* ROGER *takes another look at his document.*)

LUCINDA. Here you are, now. Here's your wine. (*Places carafe on table.*) What are you after doing now, Miss Nora? Chewing like a dog with a bone.

NORA. It's allowed in Europe.

LUCINDA. Yes, by those *I*talians! They would do that now, wouldn't they?

ROGER. Miss Nora is old enough to please herself, Lucinda.

LUCINDA. Is she indeed! Very well. Here's your medicine. (*She puts tray on table* L.) You'd better be taking it.

ROGER. What? Oh, thank you.

(LUCINDA *pours water for* ROGER.)

LUCINDA. *And* you'll be having water, Mr. Roger. If you want anything else would you ring, please?

ROGER. Yes, we'll ring.

LUCINDA. Thank you, sir. And I knows when I'm not wanted any more.

ROGER. What's that?

LUCINDA. I said nothing at all. Don't you forget that medicine.

(LUCINDA *goes.* ROGER *pours back the water and takes wine.*)

NORA. Roger!

ROGER. I am in fighting mood today. There. Your health.

NORA. And yours! Yours especially! Most urgently! Dear Roger . . . !

ROGER. You're just in time to save me.

(They drink.)

NORA. Um, delicious! I had all my things sent to Mrs. Keith's. All my bags and portmanteaux. As soon as you give me a proper invitation I shall have them sent round—that is, when you're well enough.

ROGER. No. I do not invite you, Nora.

NORA. Why not? *Pourquoi, monsieur?*

ROGER. I want you as a visitor, of course.

NORA. Not as a resident?

ROGER. No. Not yet. I'm putting this very badly.

NORA. I think I understand, Roger. You want me to start some work? Earn my own living?

ROGER. No, no.

NORA. I can, you know.

ROGER. I mean to say that I don't want you back—not yet. Not into the house. You see, I have a reason.

NORA. What is the reason, pray?

ROGER. I will tell you. I shall ask Mrs. Keith to let you stay with her a little while longer. You see, I no longer wish to be in the position of guardian to you.

NORA. Why not?

ROGER. I want you to cease to be my ward. I want you to forget your wardship. Everything.

NORA. How can I? I'm grateful for it.

ROGER. That does you credit. But gratitude mustn't weigh unduly. I never had any legal hold on you. But now I've made arrangements so that you need never feel dependent on me, or anyone. There is a document here, properly executed, which gives you this house, and a fair income. You now have absolute freedom of choice.

NORA. Why have you done this?

ROGER *(rising)*. I must tell you.

NORA. You ought not to walk about.

ROGER. I must. This is very important. *(He crosses to fireplace.)* Listen. I have waited a long time to say this to you. When I adopted you, I made up my mind to make a reasonable woman of you—as near perfection as was humanly possible. I felt that someday it would not be too difficult to make you like me—and I mean like in the strongest possible sense of the word—even to the point of affection—even if one had to put it into a single precise word—to *love* me. Don't misunderstand. I don't ask too much. Just that you should be able to care for me a little. I hope that time has now arrived. This is the question. I stake all on this. Will you come back here to me—back to this house—as my wife?

NORA. As your wife!

ROGER. Are you surprised?

NORA. Yes.

ROGER. Is it so incredible?

NORA. I had no idea . . .

ROGER. I kept it from you—naturally . . .

NORA (*rising*). Why must we change? What you've given me was so good and safe. I need you . . . I've no one else . . .

ROGER. I offer you my hand—myself—everything I possess —in marriage.

NORA. Roger—please, dear Roger . . . I thank you from my heart. You've given me so much—too much—already. I'll do anything for you on earth. But . . .

ROGER. Yes?

NORA. How can I say it? You'll think me so unkind. But —marry any woman you please . . . I'll be her serving maid —anything . . . but I can't . . . not *you*! (*She holds him and drops her head against his arm.*) No . . . I don't mean that! Dear Roger! Oh!

ROGER. I understand.

NORA. You give me no chance. No chance to think or explain . . .

ROGER. No. There's nothing to explain. I thought you might have learned to love me.

NORA. Do you mean that all this time—when I didn't know—you were teaching me to be your wife? That I was kept in the dark? I was part of a bargain? Did Mrs. Keith know?

ROGER. Yes. She knew.

NORA. And Hubert?

ROGER. I told them both. No one else. Not even Lucinda.

NORA (*suddenly resentful*). Oh, Roger!

ROGER. They kept the secret. I know they kept the secret.

NORA. But they knew you had me on a chain!

ROGER. No!

NORA. Oh, yes, you had! I see now. It was cruel of you, Roger. You talked of freedom—you let me see the world. . . . It was like letting me hear fine music and then telling me I must never listen again.

ROGER. My dear girl, that's nonsense. I have given you complete freedom of choice.

NORA. Why didn't you tell me? Why did you send me away?

ROGER. It was to give you a chance.

NORA. A chance for what?

ROGER. To find out.

NORA. What was I to find out, Roger?

ROGER. Whether you loved me or not. It seems that you don't.

NORA. I do, I *do*!

ROGER (*eagerly*). Then . . . ?

NORA. But not as your wife. You're my guardian. Why won't you understand? Oh, Roger, please . . . !

(NORA *covers her face and runs from the room.* ROGER *goes unsteadily to the bell and rings it. He replaces the document in the envelope. He is terribly shaken. There is a knock. He sits at his desk.*)

ROGER. Come in!

(LUCINDA *appears.*)

LUCINDA. Is everything all right? Where is Miss Nora?

ROGER. I don't know.

LUCINDA. Did you enjoy your meal?

ROGER. No.

LUCINDA. You must take your medicine, sir.

ROGER. Please leave me.

(LUCINDA *goes.* ROGER *is very distressed.* ISABEL *enters quickly, closing the door firmly.*)

ISABEL (R C). Roger! What happened? What have you said? Why has Nora run upstairs . . . in floods of tears?

ROGER. Because I have asked her to do me the honour of being my wife.

ISABEL. You idiot!

ROGER. You agreed . . .

ISABEL. Not so soon. We've only just arrived. What did she say?

ROGER. She declined.

ISABEL (*full of pity*). Oh, Roger!

(*She puts her hands on his shoulders.*)

ROGER. The idea seemed to horrify her.

ISABEL. I've done my best for you.

ROGER. I know you have. What does it matter? A dream shattered, that's all. An illusion . . .

ISABEL. Poor Roger . . . ! All the same, you do choose ridiculous times for proposing, don't you? I remember how *I* suffered!

ROGER. It seemed as good a time as any.

ISABEL (*crossing round table* C). There is a time and a place. Why didn't you wait?

ROGER. I told her I had been in love with her for many years.

ISABEL. Shouldn't she be just the least bit in love with you?

ROGER. I didn't demand that.

ISABEL. It is helpful. She is not unused to proposals of marriage, you know. Romantic proposals—in Rome—in Venice.

ROGER. They have turned her head.

ISABEL. You're wrong. She refused them all. She said first she must come home and find out who she really is. She has that strange American obsession with family—the people she came from.

ROGER. Are you sure there's no one else?

ISABEL. She would have none of them. Only . . . there is of course one . . .

ROGER. Who?

ISABEL. Can't you guess? Dear Roger, you are so celestially simple! Your Cousin Hubert is not.

ROGER. Hubert! Is he the man?

ISABEL. He has been, shall we say, dancing attendance on her.

ROGER (*rising*). Seriously?

ISABEL. Ever since we came off the boat. The air of New York is very intoxicating.

ROGER. Hubert—and Nora! The fellow isn't to be trusted.

ISABEL. No. That may be part of his attraction.

ROGER (*picking up the envelope*). Have I done all this for Hubert?

ISABEL. Not if I can help it.

ROGER. The first thing is that she must be happy.

ISABEL. With Hubert?

ROGER. She must be free to choose. If she loves Hubert she must marry him. I have settled an income on her.

ISABEL. Settled a fiddlestick! Unselfishness is a wonderful virtue—but we can all have too much of it. You willing to let Hubert have Nora—and I willing to let Nora have you . . .

(ISABEL *stops suddenly.*)

ROGER. Why shouldn't Nora have me?

ISABEL. My strong maternal instinct for her might have chosen a millionaire. Or a duke.

ROGER. Oh, I know. I'm an unromantic figure. I am neither handsome, nor dashing, nor celebrated. I'm sure she can find a dozen pretty lovers who are.

ISABEL. Hubert can make love eloquently.

ROGER. Can he?

ISABEL. He is an eloquent man. And he chooses his time. The evening with the lights low and music playing. Not over a piece of cold chicken in a dressing-gown! Was there ever such a lover as you?

ROGER. I have deliberately refrained from making love. Besides, it isn't the lover—it's the husband that counts. (*He takes a dictionary from the shelf.*) Husband—that's the test. Husband, husband, husband . . . The very connotation of the word. Doesn't she know what it means? (*He reads*) *The farmer who husbands his crops—the husbandman in his vineyard . . . ?* I have brought her to maturity . . . husbanded her. . . . I hoped she might see a certain rough propriety in it. Was I wrong?

(ISABEL *takes away the book and slams it down.*)

ISABEL. Oh, Roger, Roger! You can't go wooing with a dictionary.

ROGER. What's wrong with me, then?

ISABEL. I'll tell you. You have been too good—too god-like for her.

ROGER. Yes, I've watched over her—created her, almost.

ISABEL. Women don't like to be created, Roger. We are the creators.

ROGER. Did you feel the same when I asked you to marry me?

ISABEL. Yes.

ROGER. And you had no regrets? About refusing me?

ISABEL (*crossing* D C). I regretted it long before I reached the altar.

ROGER. You never told me.

ISABEL. Would I write and tell you? Send you a telegram, perhaps?

ROGER (*going to her*). But you never loved me.

ISABEL. Of course I loved you.

ROGER. Then, Isabel . . . ! Why, why . . . ?

ISABEL. You offered me everything—except one thing . . .

ROGER. What was that?

ISABEL. Danger. The disreputable. I chose the man in Rome because it seemed a great adventure. I didn't think I needed what you had to offer—safety, goodness, respectability. Now I grow old and ask for nothing else.

ROGER. Is that how a young woman's mind works?

ISABEL. You'd be surprised, Roger.

(*A knock as* LUCINDA *enters urgently*.)

LUCINDA. Mr. Roger!

ROGER. What is it?

LUCINDA. She's gone.

ROGER. Gone?

ISABEL. Nora?

LUCINDA. I heard the carriage drive away and I went to her room. She wasn't there. I found this letter for you, sir. She's gone with Mr. Hubert.

ROGER. Hubert? Did you say Hubert? I'm going after her.

ISABEL. You can't do that!

LUCINDA. It'll kill you, sir.

ISABEL. Roger, you're an invalid! This is ridiculous!

LUCINDA. Oh, ma'am, don't let him go!

ISABEL. All right, Lucinda.

(LUCINDA *goes*.)

ROGER (*reading*). Listen to this: "Dear Roger . . . I am going with Hubert . . . back to New York. I can never repay all you have done for me. I beg you not to follow me. . . ." Do you hear that? She says not to follow her.

ISABEL. I should take her at her word.

ROGER. Who would have thought Hubert was such a scoundrel!

ISABEL. He knows you have settled an income on her.

ROGER. Do you think that's what he's after?

ISABEL. That—and a pretty girl. You can withdraw the settlement. (*She sees the bottle*.) Is this your medicine?

ROGER. I must go after her!

ISABEL (*stopping him*). Sit down, Roger. You are going nowhere today. It says one teaspoon—after meals.

ROGER. I haven't had a meal.

ISABEL. It doesn't matter.

ROGER. I don't want the damned stuff! I never imagined she would do this.

ISABEL. Nor I. Open.

(ROGER *turns and swallows the medicine unexpectedly*.)

ROGER. Filthy stuff! (*He takes a drink of wine and prepares to sit* L *of table*.)

ISABEL. There. That's better. You are much too good for her, Roger. You are much more than she deserves. Now sit there, and rest.

ROGER (*jumping up*). No, I won't! Damn the girl! Damn her! Damn her! Damn her! I do beg your pardon, Isabel. . . .

ISABEL. Quite right. I don't blame you.

ROGER. I refuse to follow her. (*He sits* C.) I shall let her go. Hubert! I ought to have seen it before. She must go her own **way.**

ISABEL. And what are *you* going to do?

ROGER. I? I shall go round the world again.

ISABEL. But, Roger, you've been round the world once!

ROGER. This time I shall go in the opposite direction.

CURTAIN

END OF ACT THREE, SCENE ONE

ACT III

SCENE 2

Ten days later. Afternoon.

Baggage, a hat box, trunk and a box of books are lying around.

A large trunk stands C *where the table used to be and another* D R C *with a pile of books to* R *of it.*

LUCINDA *shows in* HUBERT.

LUCINDA. Are you expected, sir?

HUBERT (*going* D R *and taking in the disarray of the room*). Yes. He sent me a telegram.

LUCINDA. You're not popular, Mr. Hubert.

HUBERT (*picking up the legal document that lies on the desk*). No? (*He throws down the document.*) Where is he now?

LUCINDA. He went out riding.

HUBERT. Riding?

LUCINDA. He says he must strengthen his muscles. He's just changing his clothes. Are you sure you're welcome, sir?

HUBERT. I hope so. He ordered me to come and see him.

LUCINDA. I wouldn't be in your shoes, Mr. Hubert. This last ten days he's been raging like the Seven Kings of Ulster thimselves.

HUBERT (*crossing to fire and indicating trunks*). What's all this?

LUCINDA. He's going in the morning.

HUBERT. Going?

LUCINDA. Off on his travels again, sir. You will take care how you speak to him, won't you? (ROGER *enters.*) It's Mr. Hubert, sir.

ROGER (*ominously*). Thank you, Lucinda. (LUCINDA *goes quickly.*) Well? Where is she?

HUBERT. I don't know.

ROGER. You don't know!

HUBERT. She left me.

ROGER. When?

HUBERT. As soon as she arrived in New York.

ROGER. Is that all you care? You abducted her!

HUBERT (*going* C). I did not abduct her. I had no wish to abduct a girl like Nora.

ROGER. Do you mean she's not good enough for you?

HUBERT. I mean I didn't think of it.

ROGER. You ran away with her.

HUBERT. I did not run away with her. She asked for my help—to escape from you.

ROGER. What right had you to interfere?

HUBERT. You once asked me to stop you making a fool of yourself. I thought this was an appropriate occasion.

ROGER. You were flirting with the girl.

HUBERT. I only treated her as a young girl expects to be treated—with a little gaiety, a little romance.

ROGER. Were you successful?

HUBERT. No. Any little hope I may have entertained of a romantic attachment was soon dissipated—on the Boston and New York Railroad. By the time we reached Pawtucket she was definitely hostile. By New Haven she wasn't speaking at all. In New York she left me standing on the sidewalk.

ROGER. And where is she now?

HUBERT. Who can tell?

ROGER. Have you no idea at all where she might be?

HUBERT. I have an odd suspicion. If you will listen calmly and not behave like a prosecuting counsel, I'll try to tell you. I think I saw George Fenton this morning.

ROGER. Fenton!

HUBERT. We travelled on the same train.

ROGER. Do you mean she would go back to him?

HUBERT. Nora spoke of finding her own people. I just wondered.

ROGER. Why should Fenton want to come here?

HUBERT. For your blessing? Or for blackmail?

ROGER. If he does I shall send for the police.

HUBERT. Isabel has already informed the police about Nora.

ROGER. Thank God you met Isabel.

HUBERT. She is a very wonderful woman. You owe much to her.

ROGER. I know. I know.

HUBERT. She came to my office. We searched the hospitals together. We even went to the morgue. That was a memorable experience.

ROGER. The morgue—how horrible! By the way, where is Isabel?

HUBERT (*hesitating*). I'm afraid I can't tell you.

ROGER. You mean you've lost them both!

(HUBERT *picks up the document off the desk*.)

HUBERT. No. She went off to follow up an important clue. Then I received your telegram—and here I am. You ought to destroy this settlement at once. Tear it up.

ROGER (*rising*). I shall do nothing of the sort. (*Taking it*.) That's my part of the bargain.

HUBERT. And what if she doesn't keep her part?

ROGER. She is under no obligation to marry me. I told her so. I will not dominate a woman by the power of money. I am leaving for Europe in the morning.

HUBERT. I wonder why you idealists make things so difficult?

ROGER. I obey my own code of conduct.

HUBERT. More important that women should obey *you*.

ROGER. You're medieval, Hubert! Medieval!

HUBERT. So are women, Roger.

(LUCINDA *knocks and appears*.)

LUCINDA. Mr. Roger . . . ?

ROGER. Well?

LUCINDA. Mr. Fenton is here.

ROGER. Where is he?

LUCINDA. I put him in the morning-room, sir. (*Holding up the key*) I have the key.

ROGER. Fenton! (*He looks at* HUBERT.) Yes. Show him in when I ring.

(LUCINDA *goes*.)

HUBERT. You had better leave him to me.

ROGER. No! I don't trust you any more than I trust him. If he has done any harm to that girl I think I shall kill him!

HUBERT (*going to window*). Remember—your code of conduct. Nothing medieval.

ROGER. I can manage him myself, thank you.

HUBERT. May I advise complete calm?

ROGER. Please leave me. Hide yourself.

HUBERT. Equanimity, Roger. Equanimity. Remember the Ancient Greeks. If you need your lawyer I shall be out there —on the piazza.

(HUBERT *goes out through the window.* ROGER, *after ringing the bell, sits at the desk and prepares himself.* LUCINDA *appears.*)

LUCINDA. Mr. Fenton.

(GEORGE *appears jauntily.*)

GEORGE. Ah. How do you do, sir? Well? I expect you're surprised to see me.

ROGER. Have you some news for me?

GEORGE. I think I have.

ROGER. Of Nora?

GEORGE. Yes, sir!

ROGER. Then tell me where she is.

GEORGE (*enjoining caution*). Gently! All in good time.

ROGER. Pray be seated.

GEORGE. Thank you. (*He takes a cigar from box on table.*) Allow me, dear sir. I remember this room. But I think this time I hold the cards, Mr. Lawrence.

ROGER (*impatient*). Where is she? Tell me that.

GEORGE. If I have come here to oblige you, you must let me take my own way. You don't suppose I have rushed to meet you for the pleasure of the thing. In the first place there is something I must make quite clear. I owe it to Nora to tell you—that I have come here without her knowledge.

(*He sits other side of desk.*)

ROGER. If all you want to do is to torture me, why don't you say so? Tell me. Is she well? Is she safe?

GEORGE. Safe? The safest creature in the city, sir. A delightful home, maternal care, every convenience.

ROGER. Thank you.

GEORGE. Don't mention it.

ROGER. Very well. Nothing remains except that I should see her.

GEORGE. Nothing. Except one thing.

ROGER. What's that?

GEORGE. She particularly objects to seeing you.

ROGER. Possibly. That is for her to say.

GEORGE. She has said it.

ROGER. All the same, I claim the right to take the refusal from her own lips.

GEORGE. Don't you think you've had refusals enough? How you must enjoy them! (*Lights cigar.*)

ROGER. Mr. Fenton—let's not waste words! I'll try not to lose my temper. You see before you a desperate man. Come on, make the most of me. I want your help. I am even willing to be fleeced—because I know you won't do it for nothing.

GEORGE. How do you know I won't do it for nothing? I may be more of an angel than you think.

ROGER. It is unlikely.

GEORGE. All the same, my assistance may be worth something. I mean—we're all criminals at heart, aren't we? (*He leans across desk.*)

ROGER. What the devil do you mean?

GEORGE. You see, I know your story. Nora told me everything.

ROGER. Did she?

GEORGE. Oh, yes, we had a great talk. You proposed— she refused you. You planned to make her your wife years ago. You offered her money, luxury—even a settlement without any conditions.

ROGER. Did she tell you that?

GEORGE. Everything, my dear sir. She liked you—she pitied you—but she refused you flat. Reflect on that.

ROGER. I have reflected quite enough. That's over. I am her guardian. I am interested only in her welfare.

GEORGE. Very creditable. Now let me tell you my story. Excuse my egotism. Imagine, if you can, how a man placed as I am feels towards a woman.

ROGER. Do you mean she's in love with you?

GEORGE. You've hit it, sir. I am the man—the happy man. Damn it, sir, it's not my fault. Hang it, sir, I am playing the part of a saint. Nevertheless, I don't answer for myself. A man can't be a saint every day in the week. Talk about conscience when a beautiful girl sits gazing at you through a mist of tears!

ROGER (*rising*). I don't believe it!

GEORGE. Oh, you have only yourself to thank for it all. A year ago last Christmas. That was the time. If you hadn't treated me like a swindler, Nora would have been content to treat me like a friend. . . . But women have a fancy for an outlaw. . . . You turned me out of doors, and Nora's heart went with me. It has followed me ever since. Here I sit with my ugly face and hold the heart of a beautiful woman in my hand. As I say, I don't quite know what to do with it. Being an honourable man, I come to you. You propose an arrangement. I inquire your terms. A man loved is a man listened to. (ROGER *sits again*.) Now, look! If I were to say to Nora tomorrow, when I go back to New York, " My dear girl, you have made a mistake. You are in a false position. Go back to Mr. Lawrence at once, and then we'll talk about it!" Then she would sigh—she would gather herself up like a princess on trial for treason—remanded to prison—and she would march to your door. Once she's within it, it's your own affair. That's what I can do. Now what can you do? Come on— something handsome! Five thousand dollars . . . ? Make an offer then.

ROGER. You haven't even the grace to lie decently! Tell me she's ill—tell me she's lost—tell me she's dead—but don't tell me she can look at you without horror!

GEORGE. You'd be surprised!

ROGER. What are you insinuating? That you're her lover and she's your mistress?

GEORGE. No, no! You don't understand. Only that being a saint is a great strain on a man. You wouldn't like her to come home not quite the innocent who left you, would you?

(ROGER *picks up a riding whip*.)

ROGER (*rises*). Damnation! I will not suffer this infernal blackmail!

GEORGE. Careful what you say about blackmail. (*Rises.*) Didn't you try to blackmail that girl into marrying you? By giving her everything she had—and feeding her up and hoping she'd drop like a ripe peach in your hand. If that isn't blackmail I don't know what is.

ROGER. Mr. Fenton! Let me tell you what I'm going to do. I am going to horsewhip you. . . .

(*The whip lash is caught in a knot.*)

GEORGE. Ha, ha! Not to within an inch of my life?
ROGER. Yes, sir!
GEORGE. Oh, no, kind sir!

(GEORGE *leaps over trunk.* HUBERT *enters by the window.*)

HUBERT. What's going on in here? (ROGER *threatens* GEORGE. HUBERT *holds* ROGER.) Roger, what are you doing?
GEORGE. He's horsewhipping me! He isn't doing it very well.
HUBERT. Roger! Don't be ridiculous!
ROGER. This fellow threatens to seduce Nora. It's blackmail!

(HUBERT *takes the hunting crop from* ROGER.)

HUBERT. May I take this from you, please? May I also take charge of the case? You understand there is a legal aspect of blackmail, Mr. Fenton?
GEORGE. Well? He wouldn't dare go to the law. I can tell you that. He couldn't face the exposure.
HUBERT. What exposure?
GEORGE. A guardian who takes a young girl into his care and then can't keep his hands off her! Isn't that true?
ROGER. No, sir! It is not true!

(HUBERT *forces* ROGER *into a chair.*)

HUBERT. Steady, Roger. You must let me call further evidence. No fighting, please. (HUBERT *goes to window and calls off.*) Will you step this way, please. I have here a witness, gentlemen, who might be described as a " goddess out of the machine ". Actually she's out of the 10.15 from New York. Will you come in, please. (ISABEL *appears.*) You see, Mr. Fenton, there were more passengers on that train than you and I were aware of.
ROGER (*rising*). Isabel! Is Nora safe?
ISABEL. Yes, Roger, she's quite safe. I found her in that

very cheap lodging-house where you had hidden her, Mr. Fenton.

GEORGE. I can explain all that.

ISABEL. Is he asking for money?

ROGER. He is.

ISABEL. Ah, that makes blackmail as well. I've already told the police about the unlawful detention, Mr. Fenton.

GEORGE. She doesn't know what she's talking about.

ISABEL. Oh, yes, she does. I made inquiries about you, Mr. Fenton. You don't have a very good record.

GEORGE. But, lady, I *am* her cousin. I'm something that belongs to her.

ROGER. Well, she can have you! Ring the bell, Hubert. We must decide what to do.

GEORGE. Look, Mr. Lawrence, I need capital—you need the girl. I could make my business very big—and that's a fine American thing to do, don't you think?

ROGER. We shall meet again. In court.

HUBERT. Naturally, you must prosecute. The law will take care of him.

GEORGE. Wait a minute. Blackmail, unlawful detention, false pretences. I make an interesting case, don't you think?

HUBERT. You do. I advise a good lawyer.

GEORGE. You wouldn't consider . . . ?

HUBERT. No, I wouldn't. I shall be acting for Mr. Lawrence.

(LUCINDA *appears*.)

ROGER. Lucinda—Mr. Fenton will await further instructions. Put him in the dining-room.

LUCINDA (*taking key from apron pocket*). Yes, sir. I will, sir. (*She holds up the key reassuringly.*) Come on with you!

GEORGE. Don't forget, Mr. Lawrence. I still hold all the best cards. A regular handful.

(*He follows* LUCINDA.)

ROGER. Hubert—you had better go with him.

HUBERT. I will indeed.

ROGER. And send for the police.

(HUBERT *goes out after* FENTON.)

ROGER (*clenching his fists impotently*). Oh, I ought to have knocked the fellow senseless!

ISABEL. Roger, please calm down. I have something to tell you.

ROGER. He had the impudence to demand five thousand dollars.

(*He strides to the brandy and pours a glass shakily.*)

ISABEL. Which I hope you very properly didn't pay him.

ROGER. He talked to me as though we were fellow criminals.

ISABEL. Roger—do you think you ought to drink?

ROGER. I ought to have drunk a great deal more. That's what's wrong with me. No determination. I am not a man of the world. In spite of having been round it.

(*He drinks as though taking medicine.*)

ISABEL. Don't you want to hear about Nora?

ROGER. No! I never want to hear about her again. (*He drinks.*) Does . . . is she . . . in love with this man?

ISABEL. Roger—Nora is here.

ROGER. Here?

ISABEL. I brought her with me on the train.

ROGER. Nora?

ISABEL (*pointing through window*). She is at this moment sitting out there on the piazza.

ROGER. What does she say?

ISABEL. She hasn't spoken a word since we left New York. I've spent seven hours in the train with a girl who might have been a lump of cooking fat for all I could get out of her.

ROGER. Ah! So she's defiant, is she?

ISABEL. I think she's ashamed.

ROGER. I knew it! She has been seduced!

ISABEL. You are to believe nothing that man told you.

ROGER. He hinted at the unspeakable.

ISABEL. Utterly untrue. Even a scoundrel doesn't want to spoil the market value of what he has to sell.

ROGER. You mean she's left him, then?

ISABEL. I wouldn't be too sure. He has only to raise a finger and she'll go back to him.

ROGER. That's what the scoundrel said. Very well. (*Rises.*) I never want to set eyes on her again.

(He goes for another drink. His speech is a little slower but he has no sign of intoxication.)

ISABEL. Roger, you know that isn't good for you. And you must see the girl.

ROGER. No! I've wasted enough time on her already. Oh, don't think I'm not grateful to you, Isabel. You found her and you brought her home. You kept your promise.

ISABEL. Yes, I have kept all my promises.

ROGER. Won't you have just a little drink?

ISABEL. No, thank you! You know I never do. And it's very unlike *you*.

ROGER *(softening)*. You're a very remarkable woman, Isabel.

ISABEL. Thank you very much.

ROGER. I have something of importance to say to you.

(He kneels beside her.)

ISABEL *(dismayed)*. Oh, dear . . .

ROGER. Isabel. I offered to marry you once.

ISABEL. Three times.

ROGER. Three times? Yes. I feel it is now my duty to repeat the offer.

ISABEL. No, Roger! *(Rises and crosses D L.)*

ROGER. Are you sure?

ISABEL. Quite sure. You think people are isosceles triangles or something. That love is a proposition in geometry. It doesn't work that way. Besides, you're too late again.

ROGER. Too late?

ISABEL. Hubert has proposed to me.

ROGER *(angry)*. Hubert! Not Hubert again? Where? With the lights low and the music playing, I suppose?

ISABEL. Actually it was on the steps of the morgue. He was very eloquent. He has promised to repeat it in more congenial surroundings.

ROGER. I knew Hubert wasn't to be trusted.

ISABEL. I don't know what I should have done without him in New York.

ROGER. Evidently! Well, you can have him now. For good. You can all go away and leave me. I shall end my days here—as an old man—entirely alone. I shall never marry anybody.

(He is looking out of the window.)

ISABEL. That's for you to choose, Roger. But I do think you ought to speak to the girl. After all, you are her guardian.

ROGER. Her guardian, yes. That was the trouble. Look at her—sitting there. So innocent. How could she do this to me?

ISABEL. If you don't want her to run away again you had better stop her. You *are* responsible for her morals, you know. She'll probably go and live with him.

ROGER. No, by heaven! I won't let that scoundrel have her. I won't! I won't! I won't!

(*He goes to the drawer of his desk and takes the cash box.*)

ISABEL. What are you going to do?

ROGER. I'm going to settle his hash for him!

ISABEL. You mean you're going to pay him?

ROGER. Leave him to me.

ISABEL. You have no need to pay him a cent if you'll only wait for the police.

ROGER. I could strangle him!

ISABEL. Roger! No violence. Please! He might turn out to be stronger than you.

ROGER. I shall be ruthless with him. You'll see, I shall be a match for him.

ISABEL. Dear Roger! Do be careful. Keep on the right side of the law, whatever you do.

ROGER (*snapping his fingers*). The law? I don't care *that* for the law!

(*He turns back for a quick drink, emptying what is left in the glass. Then he goes out.* ISABEL *goes to the window and calls to* NORA. HUBERT *returns.*)

ISABEL (*calling*). Nora! Nora, come in. Don't be stupid! Come inside! (*To* HUBERT.) Why have you left them?

HUBERT. He has asked me to leave him alone with the man.

ISABEL. Is that wise?

HUBERT. It's very worrying. He seems to be over-excited.

ISABEL. You ought to have stayed with him. As his legal adviser. Heaven knows what he'll do. What's happening?

HUBERT (*listening*). They're very quiet. I can't hear a word.

ISABEL. You ought to be ready to give assistance.

HUBERT. I wonder what's going on?

ISABEL. He may need your help.

(HUBERT *closes door*. NORA *comes in at the window*.)

NORA. Did you call me?

ISABEL. Yes, you may be wanted. (*Leads her to chair by desk*.) You may have to decide what is to be done in a very difficult situation. Sit down. George Fenton has come here to try to get money out of Roger. It is his price for sending you home. Now do you realise the sort of man you ran away with? (NORA *is silent but shaken*.) Well, surely you can speak?

NORA. I have nothing to say.

ISABEL. As the cause of all this trouble I do think you might be more helpful.

NORA. Why don't you let me go?

ISABEL. Because you are my responsibility.

(*A voice in the hall*.)

HUBERT (*at the door*). There they are.

NORA. Let me go!

ISABEL (*holding her shoulder*). Sit still! (*A door slams*.) What's that?

HUBERT. He's coming.

ISABEL. Yes, but which one? (ROGER *appears*.) Roger! Are you all right?

ROGER. Yes. Thank you.

HUBERT. Where is he?

ROGER. Gone.

ISABEL. Where?

ROGER. Back to where he came from.

HUBERT. For good?

ROGER. He will not return.

HUBERT. Did you get a receipt?

ROGER. What for?

HUBERT. For the money?

ROGER. No.

HUBERT. Always get something in writing. Especially when dealing with scoundrels.

ISABEL. Here is Nora.

ROGER (*coldly*).   How do you do?

(*He turns away, putting cash box on piano.*)

ISABEL.   Before we go, may Hubert and I have the use of the dining-room also?

ROGER.   Certainly, if you wish.

ISABEL.   It is so much more congenial than the morgue. (*She turns to* NORA.)   You are very welcome to come to my house, Nora. But first of all I am sure Roger has something to say to you.

ROGER.   I have nothing whatever to say to her.

ISABEL.   Then perhaps Nora has something to say to *you*. She could at least apologise.

NORA (*stiffly*).   I am much obliged to you, Mrs. Keith.

ISABEL.   My dear Nora, you will probably never know how much you are obliged to me. It is a most peculiar obligation. Isn't it, Roger? Come, Hubert.

(ISABEL *goes.* HUBERT *follows. There is silence.* ROGER *is on his dignity. He starts to pack the books again.* NORA *speaks with difficulty.*)

NORA.   Mr. Lawrence . . .

ROGER.   Well? What is it?

NORA.   I am sorry for all the trouble I've caused.

ROGER.   No. There's no need. I am probably just as much to blame. (*He is on his knees at the chest.*) Will you please hand me the pile of books on the corner of the desk? Thank you. You understand that things can never be quite the same again?

NORA (*rising and handing books*).   I understand.

ROGER (*coldly*).   Why did you go?

NORA.   I told you once. A strange feeling . . .

ROGER.   What strange feeling?

NORA.   That I'm nobody. That I don't really belong to anybody. I wanted to go back again to the beginning . . . where you found me . . . in that hotel in New York. That's where I remember my father. That's why I wanted to go back.

ROGER.   Did you find it? The hotel?

NORA.   It wasn't there. They've pulled it down.

ROGER.   Well, I hope you're satisfied. Of course I admit

it may be all my fault. I probably seemed offensive to you.
Here, I want you to take this, and keep it. It gives you
complete independence. (*He gives her the legal document.*)
And I would like you to realise that this is not blackmail.
I am making no conditions. I shall be going away for a long
holiday. Round the world. (ROGER *busies himself with pack-
ing books as he talks.*) You see, Nora, I realise now that the
relationship of a guardian, or a teacher, can never be a proper
recommendation for a husband. You can now go out into
the world. On your own. I shall understand.

NORA. Did you have to pay George a great deal of money?

ROGER. That is all over. Let us try to forget it.

NORA. He *was* a blackmailer, wasn't he?

ROGER. He called it raising capital.

NORA. How much did he want?

ROGER. If you must know, he wanted five thousand
dollars.

NORA. So that was the price he put on me.

ROGER. Don't worry. I paid him no money whatsoever.

NORA. No money?

ROGER. I was too clever for him. You see, I tricked him.

NORA. You, Roger?

ROGER. I am delighted to discover that I am as diabolical
a scoundrel as your Mr. Fenton. I cheated him.

NORA. No . . .

ROGER. I cheated him—I tricked him—I bamboozled him!
Look! (ROGER *takes a pack of cards from his pocket.*) I
challenged him—to cut the cards for you.

NORA. My father's special cards!

ROGER. Yes. They worked admirably. Watch this . . .
look . . . every time . . . !

(*He cuts the pack on the lid of the trunk in front of him.
It is always an ace.*)

NORA. Roger! Dear Roger! How noble of you.

ROGER. No. It was a shameful victory. You have seen the
ugly side of my nature. Of course it is only fair to say, Nora,
that I had been drinking.

(NORA *tears the document.*)

What are you doing? You mustn't do that. It's a legal
document.

(*She lets the pages fall, and holds her head her eyes partly closed.*)

NORA (*intensely*). Roger, I have another very strange feeling!

ROGER. What's the matter?

NORA. It is a singular sensation—altogether nameless—like when the physician gave me ether.

ROGER (*concerned*). Are you quite well?

NORA. It is then that I get a full realisation of being. It is then that I begin to know the secret of the universe.

ROGER. And what is that?

NORA. That there is only one man in it with a heart.

(ROGER *rises, disgusted.*)

ROGER. Of course, if you feel like that about him you'd better go after him. (*He examines a book.*) Bishop Berkeley? I shall take him with me.

NORA. Roger—don't you understand?

ROGER. What?

NORA. One man . . . it's *you*!

ROGER (*turning*). Me? You mean . . . you have this nameless sensation about me?

NORA. Yes.

ROGER. The secret of the universe?

NORA. Yes!

ROGER. And I am the man?

NORA. Of course!

ROGER (*ecstatic*). *Hay mahnia Dionusia!*

NORA. I beg your pardon?

(*He sits on the trunk.*)

ROGER. That's what the Ancient Greeks called it. The frenzy of Dionysus. I have it too.

NORA. Oh, Roger, please take me with you.

(*She sits beside him on trunk.*)

ROGER. Where?

NORA. Patagonia.

ROGER. Patagonia?

NORA (*pointing*). Population?

ROGER. Scanty.

NORA. Climate?

ROGER. Arid.

(*The curtain is falling quickly.*)

NORA. Geographical formation?

BOTH (*shouting together*). Tertiary calciniferous basaltic!

THE CURTAIN IS DOWN.

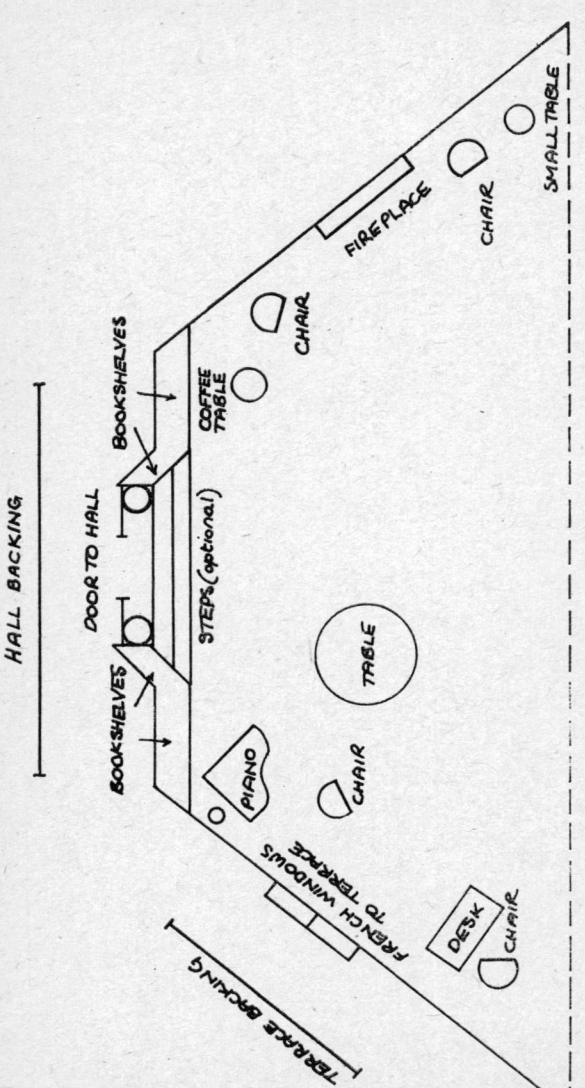

Note: Please note that the pillars either side of the door, and the steps leading down, are optional.

PROPERTY PLOT

Act I

Doors open.
Windows closed.
Piano open.

Replace C table.

Library steps behind pillar U.L.
Handmirror D.S. end of piano.
Vase on table U.L.
Desk against wall D.L.
Waste-paper basket under desk.
Globe U.S. end of desk.
Pile of notebooks U.S. end of desk.
Four leatherbound books U.S. end of desk.
Box of matches U.S. end of desk.
Box of matches on mantelpiece.
Photograph of Nora on mantelpiece.
Logs in grate.
Dictionary in bookcase U.L.
Travelling rug over desk chair.
Roger's glasses from personal to desk.

Off U.L.
Vase of flowers.
Battery oil lamp.
Silver tray with decanter of brandy and three brandy glasses.
Small tray with bottle of medicine, spoon and carafe of wine.
Medium round tray with plate of bread and cheese, apples and knife.
Large tray with two plates of chicken, potato salad and beetroot—
    two plates of rolls and butter—two wine glasses—jug of water
    —two serviettes—two large knives, two small knives, two forks—
    all on lace cloth.
One single serviette.
Large key.
Letter.
Box of cigars
Flower box—white tissue paper—lilac—blossom—loose petals.
Two large Christmas garlands—two small—red ribbon trimmed.
Scissors.
Loose green leaves.
Work box with 80 dollars, wools, scissors, trick pack of cards.
Small narrow tray with smoking cap—rack of pipes—jar of tobacco
    —matches and striker.
Valise.
Vase.
Metal cash box.
Riding whip.

Tin trunk.
Wooden wardrobe trunk.
Off D.R.
Two snowballs.
Effects.
Gong. Off U.C.
Door bell. Off U.L.
ELECTRICS.
On Stage.
Tall oil lamp on table U.L.
Desk lamp off U.L. ready to plug D.R.
Fire basket in fireplace.
Fire flicker effect behind fire basket.
Personal.
Roger: Watch and chain. Wallet with 100 dollars. Handkerchief.
Hubert: Hat and stick. Overcoat and goloshes. Watch and chain.
              Cigars in case. Legal document.
Nora: School report (put inside school hat).—Watch on ribbon.
George: Coat. Box of matches—Visiting card—Two dollars—
              Long cigars.

ACT II, SCENE 1

Curtains closed. Doors closed.
Strike.
Summer curtains and replace with winter and closed.
Bowl of flowers.
School report.
Set.
Globe, Patagonia diary, Roger's glasses on wine table L of A/C. L.
Smoking kit on tray on table U.L.
Scissors on D.S. end of mantelpiece.
Turn small ladies' chair D.L. to face in with work box below, on
    stool.
Library steps in front of fire.
Two garlands on bookshelves L and R of C doors.
Small garland on picture frame above fire D.S. end.
Small garland on ladies' chair back.
Leaves on hearth-rug.
Cash-box on desk.
Silver tray with brandy and three glasses on C table.
Exercise-books and text book on C table.
ELECTRICS.
Set and plug desk lamp D.L.
Check oil lamp U.L.
Check battery lamp off U.L.

ACT II, SCENE 2

Curtains open. Doors closed.
Strike.
Tray of brandy.
Tray plus napkin and glass from piano.

ELECTRICS.
Strike battery lamp from piano.
Set.
Red felt slippers in work-box D.L.
Valise on desk-chair D.R.
Replace smoking kit U.L.
Globe on desk, U.S. end.
Patagonia diary, text books, exercise books on desk.
Reset mirror on piano.
Roger's glasses on wine table.
Open and loop curtains.

ACT III, SCENE 1

Curtains open. Doors open.
Strike.
Garlands.
Work-basket.
Nora's cape and gloves.
Winter curtains and replace with summer.
ELECTRICS.
Strike desk lamp D.R.
Set.
Ladies' chair D.L. as Act I.
Bring desk to D.R.C. with desk chair D.R. and small chair U.L.,
   all at an angle.
Match striker on desk.
Globe on desk U.S. end.
Box of lilacs and blossom on C table.
Cigar-box with cigars on wine table L.C.
Personal.
Make Roger's glasses into personal in dressing-gown pocket.

ACT III, SCENE 2

Curtains open. Doors open.
Strike.
Centre table.
Tray of food C.
Tray of medicine from wine table.
Vase of flowers from piano.
Set.
A/C L.C. and wine table back on marks.
Wooden trunk where C table was.
Tin trunk D.L.C. with pile of books on it.
Replace dictionary.
Document and riding crop on desk D.S. end.
Cash box in drawer of desk.
Silver tray with brandy and two glasses on wine table.
Personal.
Roger's glasses from dressing gown to final suit.
Pack of trick playing cards to pocket of Roger's final suit.